A Micro Approach to Human Welfare

A Micro Approach to Human Welfare

N.N. Shrivastava

PARTRIDGE
A Penguin Random House Company

To order additional copies of this book, contact
Partridge India
000 800 10062 62
orders.india@partridgepublishing.com

www.partridgepublishing.com/india

CONTENTS

PREFACE

The suggested micro approach is alleged to be an undivided subject matter of the analytical frame work of the Economics Of Welfare. It reconciles both the cause of life and livelihood through work. It is proposed that welfare-peace and happiness can be secured through work. The accomplisher of work is an individual. It was disappointing to note that the contributions to the Economics of Welfare are macro in their approach. The issue of welfare revolves around an increase in aggregate production and its equitable distribution to improve the standard of living of the masses. An individual is reduced to be a passive receiver of welfare.

For the reason, we postulate the existence of man as a micro order. This notion is an analogue of the concept of macro order. The parameters of micro order are the Self (soul), ego, and variety of instruments contained in the body. An individual, as worker, uses the inputs provided by Self, instruments of activity endowed by nature and countless number of work material and knowledge supplied by the macro order. Now what matters most is the decision of an individual. The decision affects the design of the use of the received inputs. The decision can either improve or impair and individual's welfare. The desire born of selfish will and work managed to achieve it is argued to close in subjective constraints, psychic ups and down swings and suboptimal use of the received inputs. The decision overrun by selfish will impairs human welfare. On the contrary, work as duty adapted to improve the welfare of others, without disregarding one's own adds to welfare across-the-board. The spirit of sacrifice and selfless service evokes a set of thought contents of activity which recoils on oneself to foster welfare. The micro approach deletes the incidence of selfish will both on desire and work aspects of human activity. It is noted that, from the point of view of an individual, work after its completion and its outcome after consumption become non-existent. But the humane sprit to work leaves a lasting scar called poise. It yields a state of stable equilibrium in intelligence. It is conducive to most impartial and objective decision making. The goal of life is affirmed to be the attainment of poise-the ultimate source of peace and happiness.

The analytical framework of the theoretical construct in the present work draws heavily form the celebrated work on "Bhagwat Gita" by Swami Ramsukh Das (Gita press, Gorakhpur, 42nd Edition, 2001)—Here in referred as the text. My lack of knowledge of Sanskrit was recompensed by the progressive commentary in Hindi by Swami Ramsuhkdas and the translation of each verse contained in the text in English by Sarveapalli Radhakrishnan & Charles A. Moore in "Source Book In Indian Philosophy" (London Oxford University Press, 1957). The running matter contained in the seven chapters freely cites the Verses contained in the text. In addition to it, cross references on a section wise basis are also mentioned to build continuity in the theoretical framework of the micro approach to human welfare.

I express my gratitude to my son Naveen and Nishant Shrivastava. I was tired of watching their tireless effort to bring this work to public notice. The contribution of my wife Mrs. Usha Shrivastava, post-graduate in Economics, defies narration. Her criticism following patient listening and listening followed by criticism used to pull ideas, concepts and approach to this work form my subconscious to conscious mind in countless ways.

N.N. Shrivastava
85, Marutipuram,
LUCKNOW-226016
INDIA

*   *   *

CHAPTER-I

IN QUEST OF THE EDGE

The existence of individuals involves the issues raised by life without livelihood and livelihood without life is a misnomer of existence. The subject matter of Economics is mindful of individual's livelihood and his welfare in the context where ends are various but the means to achieve them are limited. The commendable contributions to welfare economics spring from the background of scaracity—chronic scarcity. The enhancement of production and its rational distribution encircles the contributions to welfare. The aim is to reduce income and wealth inequalities among the masses. The quest for individual's welfare persuaded us to find out what one can do to attain welfare for oneself and other selves. The micro foundations to welfare is intended, to supplement to macro approach to human welfare.

But either approach to individual's welfare is beset with two undeniable highly restrictive constraints. Prof. Robbins tells as that (I) "here we are, sentient creatures with bundles of wishes and aspirations with masses of instinctive tendencies all urging us in different ways to action". We are also made aware that (2) "the external world does not offer full opportunities for their complete achievement". The consequences of real causes are also real. Individual's life, so also his livelihood, both are ravaged by the absolute nature of economic scarcity. This kind of scarcity, all tacitly degenerates into 'chronic scarcity'. This is for the reason that the human psychology is involved before, during and after the completion of any thought and/or action. The utility gained by digesting the constraint of budget could be offset, or more than offset, by the psychic cost of chronic economic scarcity. A close associate of chronic economic scarcity is the phenomena of paucity. The obsession of paucity-that is, feeling of smallness or lack of available means continues to pester individuals, in varying degrees, at any level of poverty, or inversely affluence. The notion of paucity, thriving on the impulse of attachment and greed, often than not, overshoots all the levels of permanent real income. Individuals bear the psychic cost of economic scarcity and paucity over whole span of their life. The subjective constraint born of paucity and economic scarcity keeps the individuals, psycho-economic perspective continually suspended in an unsecure situation. The plight of man established in discomposure naturally seeks composure-equanimity. The search for solution brings us to the edge of the science of Economics. Individuals' welfare is an unfinished issue.

The concept of welfare is indicative of the well-being, as of health, happiness and prosperity. We put aside the health aspect of well-being and keep happiness and prosperity as separate but not unrelated issues. The phenomena of happiness and prosperity do not necessarily go together. Prosperity, ever increasing levels of prosperity, in substance ensures pleasure from the widening circles of the relation of concern with people, their activities and its outcome. In other words, our body and bodily concerns get merged into dimensionless world of concerns. One gets completely pre-occupied with the time bound entities. These entities come into existence to pass out of it. The time shape of their yield, whatever may be its length, tends to be finite. Work connects us with people, their activities and its outcome. But work after its completion and its outcome after its consumption becomes non-existent. In short, prosperity as indexed by the gratification of senses and accumulation of wealth makes for transient happiness. Consequently, one is bewitched by the undying urge for happiness at all the levels of prosperity. The upshot of these arguments is that our body, so also bodily concerns, guarantees only short-lived and transitory happiness. The urge for happiness continues unabated throughout the span of life. This is for the reason that we fail to identify the ways and means to attain enduring happiness. It has to be sought through work, acquisition, consumption, possession of means of comfort and concern for our near and dear ones. We need welfare in the face of all agreeable and disagreeable events, situations and circumstances. It is also well known that the gain of short-lived pleasures, so also pain, is proportional (Verse5-20) to the extent of attachment to the bodily and wordly concerns. The lack of positive correlation between happiness and prosperity signifies the search for happiness outside the orbit of attachment to the transitory entities. It implies that attachment to the everlasting entity can yield enduring happiness at any level of prosperity. The whole issue boils down to how to establish the relation of concern with an everlasting entity without renunciation in any sense whatsoever.

The issue of happiness has tacitly avoided the deliberation of 'individual' whose welfare is being sought. The existence of individuals as a living being comprises their outer being—labelled as the body and inner being—designated as the soul. In substance while the soul is endowed with, the body is devoid of, consciousness. In esssence while the soul is beginingless, everlasting and an omniscient entity, the body is a congregation of a number of entities, bound by the laws of nature, comes into existence to pass out of it. The assemblage of entities in the body is indicative of a variety of instruments of activity. Each instrument performs its functions to make human activity meaningful. The soul-alive entity sets up relations of concern with the body. The relations, thus set up, animate all entities included in the body. The contents of the body become pseudo-alive entities. Each entity performs its highly specialized and non-overlapping functions over the whole life span. This approach to the existence of individuals is conceptualized as the "micro order". The human body like a railway engine, at the instance of our decisions, uses the fuel provided by the soul through the senses, the mind, the intelligence and ego. Multitude of individuals, micro orders, when aggregated, make a macro order. It is contended that an individual monitors, so also is monitored, by, the micro order. The micro order is self-governing and self-sustained.

To apprehend the precise nature of the micro order, we think at length about the body, as nature creates and the soul, as a fraction of the Supreme Self. The soul, unlike body, is beyond change and activity. It is completely free from the flaws and shortcomings associated with change. But the soul, being the seat of consciousness, has the power to make or withdraw any relation of concern set up by himself with the body. Although, the soul sets up relation with the body, it lacks the power to act. The body, on the contrary, possesses the power to act, hence beset with change and flaws. But the body lacks the power to set up or undo the relation with the soul. It is explicitly pointed out that the soul and body are intrinsically entities of different kind. The innate nature of the soul is changelessness. The body, being nature create, embodies action and change. The relation set up by the soul with the body carries implications of immense significance. The soul comes to encounter dual relation with the body. In the first place, 'I' as the body is the identity proof of the existence of the soul. Secondly, the soul as the owner of the body is held accountable for anything that the body does. But the impulse of attachment, born of the propensity to passion, de-generates the identity of the soul into the self-sense of one's individuality. And the soul as the owner of the body spreads his ownership over work material, work itself and its outcome. In other words, the congregation of pseudo-alive entities arbitrates between the soul and the ceaseless change occurring in the entities in the world outside one self. Consequently, the soul even though beyond change appears to bear the incidence of unsettled psycho-economic perspective caused by changeability. The fact of reality poses a serious problem. How human life and livelihood, be optimally maneuvered in the face of change, A failure to do so would result in underutilization of endowments provided by the bodily and non-bodily existences.

The human ego acts as a bridge between the soul and the body. This is because ego comprises two parts—one part embodies, and the other part does not embody, consciousness. The parts of the ego respectively proxy for the soul and nature create body. Consequently, the alive part of ego experiences attraction, change and its outcome through its non-alive counterpart, which is directly involved in unceasing change in nature. The presumption of the soul to be incorporated in the body drives him to experience pain and pleasure, sorrow and joy etc. This aspect does not agree with the fact of ultimate reality. The soul, as an entity beyond change (Verse 13-13 & 13-32) acts as the basis, illuminator, hence the experience of change, seems to contradict itself—nonetheless it is a part of life reality. It implies that either the relation of concern enjoined by the soul or the working of the micro order itself unsettles its own working. We put forward the later half of the above settlement as a premise.

The preceding line of reasoning can be restated to justify the relevance of the suggested hypothesis. Theoretically the basis of attraction between two entities is the sameness of their kind. To illustrate, each sense of perception responds only to its respective object only—eyes respond to sight, not to sound. Thus the foremost cause of attraction between two entities (Verse 3-28) is their alikeness in character. This is the basic condition for attraction, urge to action and action to become a fact. It is fulfilled through and by nature born entities. The soul stands completely apart from attraction, urge to action, action and its accomplishment that materializes in nature, yet the soul is upheld (Verse 13-20) as the cause of experience of pleasure and pain. The proneness of the alive part of ego to action and change merely reflects the indulgence of the non-alive part of ego in nature. The soul despite being lodged in nature (the body) neither acts (Verse 13-31) nor gets tainted by human decisions and actions. The suggested hypothesis seems to stand unshaken. There must be some factor (s) which disfigures the original nature of the relation of concern set up by the SELF with other entities. Consequently, the soul (or the SELF) mistakenly (1) presumes to be the governor of the body including its contents and other non-alive entities. But the soul gets helpless (2) because of excessive dependence of man on non-alive entities, or entities devoid of consciousness. As a result (3) the involvement of the self in entities other than the self makes him oblivious to exploit his own potentialities. The soul despite his innate strength (Verse 15-8) to wipe out the flaws besetting the original relation of concern feels infirm to do the needful.

The above arguments point out the areas for further investigation. We start with the premise that the incompetence of the soul is virtual. The soul being an alive and self-existent entity is the prime mover of life and livelihood. It is timeless, same for ever and begeningless. The self-existent nature of the soul speaks for his being self existent and self-sustaining. The objectives of bodily relations of concern, set up by the soul, are preservation, growth and procreation of life. The tools of likes-dislikes, taste-distaste and attraction-repulsion are built into the instinctive ways of perception, thinking and decision making and action. But the actualization of the bodily relations depends upon work, accomplished by the body and its contents. Yet the facts of reality are that the body, all kinds of work material, work itself and its outcome are transient entities and devoid of consciousness. These are non-existent entities—come into existence to pass out of it. The vibrant nature of the non-existent entities is derived from the soul. The suffering is seldom caused by the non-existent entities. The real cause which upsets the natural working of the micro order (Verse 18-45) is the neglect of precepts of the Self-that is reason, insight and foresight. The real cause is not the aptitude of indulgence but the attitude of self-indulgence. The attitude driven by (Verse 3-33) attachment and aversion makes one's own personal nature impure. It defiles the natural relations of concern set up by the soul. The paradox is that one's own personal nature begins to instill rules about how to think and how to behave. The soul, being the seat of consciousness, causes the stream of active consciousness to bear the incidence of all deviations from the rules of the game. The entire perspective of the lower self (body including its contents) grows unsettled, casting its reflection on the higher self (the soul). These arguments demonstrate suffient evidence to prove that an individual can attain or impair welfare for himself.

I-2 THE CHAPTERS AHEAD

The welfare of human beings involves the issues raised by life and livelihood. We feel the need for an analytical framework that considers the issue without omitting either an individual's life or livelihood. The macro approach to welfare disregards the issues of life. The eventual need of life is poise and peace. The contributions to welfare revolve around production and its rational distribution to reduce income and wealth inequalities among the masses. This is the macro approach to the issue of welfare. The deviation from the macro approach persuaded us to enquire (Chapter-I) what an individual can do to attain welfare for himself and others. This we label as the micro approach to human welfare. It is proposed to supplement the existing contributions to the issue of welfare.

The suggested approach views the existence of human beings (Chapter-II) as a micro order. The order comprises his soul (the Self) and body. The inputs provided by the Self (consciousness, life energy and knowledge) animate the instruments of activity contained in the body. The Self, ego, instruments of activity and the nature born triad of propensities are identified as the variables controlling the working of the micro order. The qualities of thought contents produced by the instruments of activity connect the world inside with the world outside oneself.

The nature born triads of propensities are that of passion, passivity and purity. The propensity to passion activates, passivity deactivates and purity enlightens the entire sequence of human activity. The interaction (Chapter-III) between the three propensities is mirrored in the stream of active consciousness. Further, the propensity to passion is an incarnate of the impulse of attachment. The passion born impulse of attachment creeps into every impact of each propensity through human activity. The advance and retreat of the thought currents generated by the three propensities depends upon the decision of and individual. The motive fixed in selfish-will triggers off the thought currents of passion to assume a lead. Accordingly, the thought currents of purity move forward because of the motive of sacrifice and selfless service to others.

The specification (Chapters-II & III) of four variables paves the way to consider the working of stylized models of the micro order. The notion that each variable (Chapter-IV) influences and is in turn influenced by the remaining three variables constitutes the essence of working of the micro order. We find that the synchronous changes in the composition of ego and propensity-mix depend upon the nature of an individual's decision. Accordingly, the variables ego and triad of propensities emerge as the pace-setter of the micro order. This is for the reason that the Self and the instruments of activity are like parameters. The Self is an epitome of inactive consciousness and the instruments function as a machine— action without thought. As a consequence, the selfish-will impels adaptation of ego to the thought currents of passion more than the thought currents of the other propensities. This gives the ego-embodied model of the micro order. As against this, the non-appearance of selfish-will evokes the adaptation of ego to the thought currents of purity more than that of passion and passivity. This yields the egoless model of the micro order.

The next step explores the implications of the ego-embodied model of micro order. The egoism and attachment fostered by passion strengthens selfish-will. It is premised that desires (Chapter-V) and work (Chapter-VI) born of selfish-will impair human welfare. The selfish desires are indeterminate, insatiable, blur wisdom and instigate sinful actions. The thought contents induced by selfish-desires (Chapter-V) upset the natural functioning of the micro order. While the realization of selfish desires hatch greed, its frustration closes in anger and delusion. The selfish desires unsettle the state of micro order through its impact on intelligence. The attachment, egoism and selfish-will sheltered in ego violate stability in intelligence. In addition to it, the pressure of passion causes the impetuous senses to engender wavering mind, which accentuates instability in intelligence. Thus the decision motivated by selfish-will gears the entire working of the micro order to impair human welfare.

It is observed that the relations of concern constrained by selfish-will conclude (Chapter VI) in constrained human activity. It causes attachment to the self-sense of being a doer, owner of the instruments contained in the body and fruits of action. The Selfish-will also escalates the impetus to action. The various manifestations of attachment, in varying degrees in countless direction build a mechanism inside oneself to internalize attachment. This is for reason of an excessive and inexorable attachment to self-indulgence and accumulation of wealth. The internalized attachment creates subjective constraints and enhances the vulnerability to ceaselessly changing perspectives both inside and outside oneself, hence ends in suboptimal use of inputs provided by the Self and nature. Thus the interactive impact between the desires and work motivated by selfishness impairs human welfare.

The foregoing analyses point out what an individual can do to attain welfare for himself and others. We contend that one can (Chapter-VIII) attain welfare through work. Work integrates the cause of life and livelihood. An individual's aptitude to work as duty fuses the macro and micro approaches to welfare. The use of means available to an individual has to be delivered from the seize of selfish-will. It has to be used for the betterment of others without disregarding one's own. This deep-seated change in decision causes ego to adapt itself to a new propensity-mix which assigns almost the same weight to the thought currents of purity as that of passion and passivity. The changed decision creates a perspective of egolessness. This objective can be achieved by (i) minimizing the internalization of attachment and (ii) escalating its externalization outside oneself. These measures delete attachment from the urge to action and induce the thought currents of purity to run parallel to the thought currents of passion. The upsurge of purity and passion, both bereft of selfish-will, cause unconstrained assimilation of the inputs provided by the Self into the instruments of activity through the intelligence. The decisions made by intelligence come to be based upon reason rather than attachment—that is, upon insight and foresight. The decisions fix eyes on the end result of thought, speech and action. The inner self (ego, intelligence and mind) come to experience poise, or a steady-state equilibrium. It implies that attachment and aversion causing deviations from the steady-state cease to be effective. The attained poise is the most valued remainder of work after its completion and return from work after its consumption. It may be recalled that work constrained by attachment (aversion) leave a remainder of unsettled micro order. The poise also sets the stage for cultivating complete non-involvement before, during and after the completion of work. This is the essence of the art of working and optimal efficiency in work. Consequently, the egoless perspective also generates the optimal use of inputs provided by the Self and nature. The Self, as the essence of life and livelihood, ceases to be subdued by attachment to self-indulgence. It is affirmed that an individual on its own can attain poise and enduring peace.

*   *   *

CHAPTER-II

THE ANALYTICAL FRAMEWORK

An individual as a micro entity specifies our analytical framework. The existence of individuals is made up of their bodily and non-bodily existences. This is a fact of ultimate-reality. It is premised that both these kinds of existences are inseparably connected to his life and livelihood. Accordingly, these facts support us (Chapter II-1) to establish the notion of micro order. The concept draws heavily upon the facts of human existence. In a most general way, the soul (the Self, or non-bodily existence) and body (or the domain containing a variety of instruments of activity) are the two components of the micro order. The strongly ordered components (Chapter II-2) describe the portrait of the micro order. The portrait includes subtle senses, subtler inner self, and subtlest part—the soul or the Self. The Self is the epitome of individual consciousness, as the seat of subjective thought and action. The description of the micro order is followed by (Chapter II-3) an itemization of the independent variables of the order. The selection of variables follows the criterion that a change in any selected variable would induce repercussions through other variables to outline the state of mico-order. The variable selected are the Self, human ego, nature born triad of propensities and the instruments of activity contained in the domain. The specification of variables is completed by taking a note of their innate attributes. Finally, the reconsideration of variables (Chapter II-5) is intended to place them in a wider perspective. The relation of concern set up by the Self with the instruments of activity and the triad of propensities (Chapter III) determines the direction of movement of micro order. The emerging state of micro order may either impair (Chapter VI), or improve (Chapter VII) an individual's welfare.

N.N. Shrivastava

II-1 THE CONCEPT OF MICRO ORDER

An individual as the micro entity is the parameter of our analytical framework. The state of existence of individuals goes to establish the concept of micro order. The human body (called the domain of activity containing variety of instruments of activity) and the soul (or the Self) account for the state of human existence. The domain contains the inputs endowed by nature and the Self alleged to be (Verse 15-7) a fraction of the Supreme-Self also provides inputs to the domain of activity. The domain is the ultimate user of endowments of nature (called secondary human capital) and the Self (primary human capital). The mode of use of the received inputs by the domain determines the obtaining psychonomic perspective in the micro order. It is notable that the Self without the domain and the domain without the Self is an incorrect naming of the state of existence. The instruments of activity contained in the domain carry out all the conceivable economic and non-economic activities.

This result indicates that the life and livelihood of individuals both are the subject of concern of the working of micro order. Any separate consideration of life or livelihood would result in theoretical constructs far away from life-reality and ultimate-reality. We contend that the Self and nature, constituting ultimate-reality, play a significant role in shaping life-reality. But the ultimate-reality makes the life-reality as seemingly self-existent. The concept of micro order attempts to probe behind the apparently looking self-existent reality. The analysis is intended to reveal that the issue of life and livelihood can be ascribed to a few common denominators having their roots in ultimate reality. The stretching of time-length, for analytical reasons, shows that all entities operative within the micro order and outside it, are transient and short-lived in nature, except the immortal living soul. The entities other than the living soul are subject to unceasing change, transformation and destruction. These facts of the ultimate-reality point out a few lessons of utmost importance. No individual can ignore the varying size, composition and time-shape of the short-lived entities. The trends in life and livelihood both are dependent upon the ever changing entities existing both inside and outside the domain. One cannot ignore their repercussions of life and livelihood. But the state of one completely involved and the other non-involved in change is no less a relevant issue. The psychonomic perspective of one completely involved in the whirl of change—that is, totally oblivious of the qualities of changelessness, imparted by the Self, would be a like a ship without an anchor. In comparison to it, a perspective of one above and non-involved in change, can manage change more efficiently. The Self, enliver of the instruments of activity contained in the domain, infuses some qualities that can be exploited to improve one's own welfare. Failing this approach, any study would be incomplete in the sense that the analysis of change for maximizing gain and minimizing loss would impair individual's welfare. This is for reason of imperfect foresight and uncertainty of foreseen and unforeseen circumstances constantly bombarding our psychonomic perspective. The decision of an individual is all that matters in impairing or improving his welfare.

Now we can point out a few salient features of the suggested concept of micro order. In the first place, the micro order is viewed as a strongly ordered methodical arrangement of its constituent parts. For the reason the order becomes self-regulating and self-sustaining. The order contains all the potentialities to preserve, procreate human existence and enable full utilization of the endowments of the Self and nature. Secondly, the methodical arrangement, built into the micro order, in a functional sense imbues the spirit of general equilibrium. Each constituent of the micro order depends upon its every other constituent. As such change in any component induces repercussion in the remaining components of the order. In a structural as well as in a functional sense both, no component of the order exists and operates independently. The only exception to this rule is the status of the Self in the micro order. The Self is the only self-existent entity. It is the ultimate provider (Verse 10-22) of life energy and consciousness to the domain of activity. The Self enlives and acts as an illuminator (Verse 13-17) of every instrument of activity contained in the domain. The Self is an absolute entity. It is the cause of existence, and preceptor of the micro order.

The spirit of general equilibrium propels the methodical arrangement of components of the micro order. This explains the third feature of the micro order. The Self being the ultimate cause of existence, establishes a relation of concern on its own initiative, with the instruments of activity contained in the domain and the nature born triad of propensities. The instruments being devoid of consciousness do not and cannot set up relations of concern with the Self. In the same way, the self is beyond the reach of the nature born triad of propensities. However, two persons of a common relative also become relative among themselves. The thought currents of the three propensities directly impinge upon every instrument of activity. In other words, the nature born propensities influence the use of total endowments through their impact on the working of every instrument of activity. Although the Self is the ultimate cause of existence, it infuses wisdom, insight and foresight to humans to decide upon the mode of use of the total inputs received by the domain of activity. The nature born propensities at most actualize the decision.

Finally, the interaction of the micro order with the world outside it also deserves consideration. It is generally observed that the ceaseless change occurring in the world outside the micro order; force their entry into the world inside the micro order. This phenomenon disturbs (Verse 18-45) the spontaneous functioning of the micro order, impairing the welfare of individuals. Out findings reveal that the world outside the domain of activity, is nothing but a net work of entities devoid of consciousness. For this reason, these entities cannot become the cause of disturbances in the micro order. It is premised that the decision of an individual to determine the mode of use of total inputs, or human capital, can impair or improve his welfare.

II-2 THE PORTRAIT OF MICRO ORDER

The portrait of micro order incorporates a three step description. In the first step we consider the constitution and nature of the domain of activity. The second step demonstrates the influence of the Self on the domain. In the third step we deliberate upon certain tendencies caused by the coexistence of the generically poles apart entities, namely Self and the domain of activity. These tendencies of varying time length, disturb the natural functioning of the micro order.

Let us consider the constitution of the domain of activity first. The domain comprises (Verse 13-5) three kinds of instruments of activity, namely, the organs of action and the organs of perception-called the external instruments of activity. The third category of instruments comprises ego, intelligence and mind—called the internal instruments of activity. The internal instruments control the actions to the external instruments of activity. The five organs of action are that of speech, hands, feet and two organs of excretion. The five organs of perception are ears, skin, eyes, tongue and noise. The objects corresponding to the organs of perception are sound, touch, sight, taste, and smell. Accordingly, the domain of activity performs (Verse 5-9) thirteen kinds of action through its thirteen instruments of activity.

The uniquely strong ordering of the thirteen instruments of activity contained in the domain is a significant aspect of the methodical arrangement of the micro order. As one ascends from the organs of action to the external instruments of activity, and from the externals to the internal instruments of activity, and from the internals to the Self (Verse 3-42 & 3-43) the discerning power, comprehensiveness of perception, strength and the capacity to illuminate the instruments lower in order grows in an increasingly increasing manner. The senses of perception discern their respective object of sense. But the objects of the senses lack the power to comprehend the senses. The senses are independent of the objects of the senses. It is noticeable that while the objects of the senses are subject to unceasing change, the senses remain consistent and changeless. The mind is greater than the senses of perception. The senses cannot comprehend mind, but mind perceives the senses. While the power of the senses to perceive is limited to their objects, the mind can discriminate between the functioning of each sense including their respective objects. The mind is more subtle, profound, and assertive than any instrument of activity.

The mind, despite its competence, lacks the capacity to perceive intelligence. But the intelligence understands the mind. The intelligence is empowered to discern all kinds of mental states. The intelligence identifies whether the mind is steady, wavering, self-possessed or swayed by something. The field of awareness of also extends over the functioning of the senses. The power of intelligence envelops mind, the senses and the objects of the senses as well. Therefore, intelligence, beyond mind, is more resolute, stable, profound and complete as compared to any part in the micro order.

But the captain of intelligence is human ego. The ego announces intelligence to be 'my intelligence'. The ego uses intelligence as an instrument. The user of instrument lies outside the purview of intelligence. The ego is the viewer of the intelligence, mind and the senses.

Thus far we have considered the constitution of the domain in terms of its external and internal instruments of activity. But despite the methodical arrangement of the instruments in the domain, the domain it self is subject to continual change and transformation. The phenomena of change, fluctuation, transformation, beingness and non-existence are the innate nature (Verse 3-26) of all the entities born of nature comprising the domain. The episode of change ability constantly generates some or the other tendency which disturbs the natural functioning of the micro order. These tendencies are directly of indirectly (Verse 13-6) born of attachment and aversion. It is evidenced by (1) anger associated with non-fulfillment of selfish-will and agitation of ego. The joy caused by (2) agreeable circumstances and pain (3) caused by disagreeable circumstances give rise to deviations from stable psychonomic disposition. The body (4) itself experiences aliment. It is a source of disturbance. The stream of active consciousness (5) registers variety of changes caused by ever changing physical and non-physical conditions. Finally, the adaptive capacity of the inner self is also changeable, as impelled by the rise and fall of the thought currents of the triad of propensities.

Now we can take up the second step to describe the micro order. It consists of the influence of the Self over the domain of activity. The external and internal instruments of activity contained in the domain become inoperative without the support of the Self. The inputs supplied by the Self to the domain animate every instrument of activity. In addition to it, the Self is the preceptor of all the (Verse 18-18) preceptors, namely, ego, intelligence, mind and the senses. The Self is the knower of all the discerners. It is notable that the Self, being a self-existent entity, is independent of all instruments of activity. The knowledge embodied and infused by the Self into the domain is absolute in nature. In contrast, the instruments of activity contained in the domain perceive with the support of each other. The perception gained by the external and internal instruments of activity yield relative knowledge. It is imperfect and subject to revision and re-revision.

The description of the portrait of micro order in the third step, like the other steps, is equally relevant for the working of the micro order. The Self lodged in the micro order, sets up relation of concern with the body. The body is treated by the Self as ' I ' and the body to be (Verse 14-1) the property of ' I '. The subjective notions of I-ness and mine-ness shape the compatibility between two incongruous entities of totally different origins. This is for the reason that the Self is an embodiment of life energy and consciousness. It can do, or undo, any relation of concern with any entity existing either inside or outside the domain. But the fact remains that the Changeless Self coexists with body (domain of activity) assailed by change. The coexistence and attending notions of I-ness and mine-ness are natural. They do not disturb the working of the micro order. The source of all kinds of unsettled state of the micro order is a variety of individual's ulterior motives fueled by the selfish-will and egoistic disposition. As a result a bundle of non-neutral thought contents of activity interferes with the working of the micro order. Consequently, the Self completely indifferent regarding the use of its supplied inputs to the domain bears (Verse 13-20) the end products of the disturbed micro order. The end-products are in the form of thought contents (Chapter VI-4) which unsettle the disposition of psychonomic perspective. An individual faces cycles of elation and depression which interfere with rational thinking. The fact is that psychic-swings belong to and occur in the domain of activity but the feeling of oneness with the psychic swings is caused by the Self. The reason being that the entities contained in the domain are devoid of consciousness. They cannot become the cause of awareness of the psychic-swings. The notable aspect is that even though the Self causes awareness, it remains untouched by the end-products of the union with the domain.

II-3 THE SPECIFICATION OF THE VARIABLES

The foregoing sections established the relevance of the concept of micro order and deliberated upon its portrait comprising the Self and the domain of activity. Now we bring up the variables to construct (Chapter IV) a stylized model of the micro order. The criterion of specification is that each variable must be independent of the influences of individual's decision but be capable of influencing the same. The Self, as a fraction of the Supreme-Self and nature create body both are outside the scope of concern of individual's decision. It is alleged that (Verse 14-5) the nature born triad of propensities—that of purity, passion and passivity, tie down the immortal living souls to the body. This verse specifies three independent variables of the model of micro order. These are the nature born triad of propensities, the living soul (or the Self) and the body, called the domain of activity. The terms body, domain of activity and instruments of activity are interchangeably used on occasion. In other words, the three independent variables of the model are the Self (S), the triad of propensities (T) and the instruments (I) of activity. Now we go in search of the last variable. It is human ego. It is neither a creation of the Self nor of nature. It is a by product of fastening of the living soul and body by the nature born triad of propensities. The human ego (E) as a byproduct partakes the attributes of the Self and the body (instruments of activity). For this reason, at times ego takes side with the body-saying that

I am this body, and other time with the Self—saying that I am the living soul. The Self and the body respectively epitomize 'inactive consciousness' and 'unconscious activity'. The variable Self (S), despite being inactive, is the only source of life energy and consciousness. The nature born variable (I) is an embodiment of unconscious activity. The implication being that the variable (I) like a machine functions without thought. As a result the union of the Self and the body yields two highly relevant variables. These are human ego and the stream of active consciousness. The ego (E) transmutes the unconscious activity into 'conscious activity'. The ego emerges as the agent of conscious activity. The inactive consciousness comes down in the form of the stream of active consciousness. The stream reflects the thought currents disseminated by the triad of propensities, the Self, ego and instruments of activity. The stream also mirrors every change arising inside and/or outside the domain of activity. The viewer of changes is the innate attribute of the Self. In view of the hybrid nature of the stream of active consciousness, only four independent variables influencing the state of micro order are the Self (S), the triad of propensities (T), human ego (E) and instruments of activity (I).

II-4 THE ATTRIBUTES OF VARIABLES

The deliberation of the attributes of the variables is necessary for more than one reason. In the first place, the consideration sharpens introspection to attain a disciplined and settled psychonomic disposition. Secondly, the working of the micro order can be analyzed only by a precise understanding of the attributes of the variables. This is for reason that the interaction among the four variables determines the state of micro order, which either impairs or improves the welfare of individuals. Finally, the changing composition of ego, and arrangement of thought currents of the propensities coats these variables (E) and (T) with exactly opposite attributes. This phenomena has crucial implications (Chapter IV-4) & (Chapter IV-5) for the working of the micro order. The only exception to this rule is the Self. The attributes of the four variables are itemized as follows:

(1) The Self is an embodiment of knowledge, steadfastness and power of thoughts. The Self is knowledge incarnate. It infuses the devices

(Verse 10-10) to acquire knowledge through intelligence. The tools are that of understanding whose auxiliaries are awareness, discernment, grasp and insight. It addition to being the source of understanding the Self is (Verse 10-11) wisdom incarnate. The attribute of the Self is perceptible in terms of the power of foresight, the capacity to pierce with intellect to reach the inner meaning of the entities other than the Self, and power to infuse intellectual light to the internal instruments of activity. The attribute of wisdom purifies (Verse 18-16) intelligence by reason, chastity and cleanliness of thinking. The Second attribute of the Self is (Verse 2-24) & (Verse 2-25) immovability and steadiness. It helps to raise one above attraction and repulsion, hence enables to maintain balanced inner self. The Self is also attributed by immovability. This is for the reason the Self is out of reach of action and inaction and change. These attributes of the Self are reinforced by yet another attribute. It is the attribute of timelessness. For the reason the Self ceaselessly provides its inputs to the domain of activity. Finally, the Self is the ultimate source of thought power. The Self (Verse 10-4 & 10-5) is the basis, energizer, illuminator of a variety of thoughts which drive the state of micro order. This attribute is supported by the infusion of life energy and consciousness (Verse 10-22) to the entities contained in the domain. But the notable fact is that (Verse 7-12) the thought contents of activity do not contain the Self, nor the Self embodies these thought contents. It implies that the Self beyond the thoughts originating in the Self.

(2) The variable (I) contains thirteen types of highly resourceful, creative, intricate and masterly instruments. Each instrument, enlivened by the life energy and consciousness infused by the Self, performs the nature decreed specialized functions strictly in a non-overlapping manner. It is observed that the variable (I) functions like a machine—that is, action without thought. This is the essence of its being an epitome of unconscious activity. Again, the variable (I), like a machine, remains unconcerned regarding the qualities of the received input-mix and produced output-mix. The variables (S), (E) and (T) inject thought contents of activity as inputs which decide the nature of input-mix. It may be recalled that the inputs provided by the Self remains the same for ever. Therefore, the changes in the quality of thought contents imbued by the variables (E) and (T) matter much in determining

the input-mix received by the variable (I). The quality of input-mix controls the nature of output-mix produced by the variable (I). It is observed that the output-mix not only affects the operations of the variables (E) and (T)—but also reacts on the state of micro order by influencing the operation of instruments contained in the domain of activity. For this reason the harmonious adjustments between the variables (E) and (T) impel to produce (Chapter IV-4 & IV-5) either neutral or non-neutral thought contents of activity, which respectively either reveal or ellipse the impact of the Self on the micro order.

(3) The triad of propensities is the third variable influencing the working of the micro order. The propensities to passion, passivity and purity act upon intelligence and mind through ego. The propensities to passion, passivity and purity occasion their impact on the domain through the impulses of attraction, repulsion and illumination. The impulses of attraction and repulsion affect the urges to need and action both. The impulse of attraction stimulates and that of repulsion discourages the impetus to action. An excess of attraction over repulsion accelerates the impetus to action. Conversely, and excess of repulsion over attraction decelerates the impetus to action. An equality between the impulses accelerating and decelerating action close in the stationary conditions of action.

But the impulses and thought currents born of the triad of propensities become effective only when the Self sets up the relation of concern with them. As a result, one becomes highly susceptible to the exit and entry of thought currents in the stream of active consciousness. For this reason, either one adores (Verse 14-22) or abhors the rise and fall of the thought currents of a particular propensity. Accordingly, the thought currents causing elation stimulate action, similarly the thought currents causing one to shrink impel to abstain from action.

The thought currents generated by the triad of propensities cast their impact of the psychonomic disposition by influencing the output-mix produced by the instruments of activity. The thought currents of passion and passivity give rise to non-neutral thought contents of activity. The thought contents grow non-neutral when their spillover effects sustain and magnify their own created imperfections and flaws. The thought currents of purity, on the other hand generate neutral thought contents of activity, all together devoid of flaws and imperfections, hence conducive to spontaneous working of the micro order. Further, each propensity binds the Self into the domain of activity in its own way. Thus the thought currents of purity (Verse 14-6) bind the Self through the pride of being knowledgeable and motive fixed in happiness of purity. The thought currents of passion (Verse 14-7) bind the Self through attachment to work and its outcome. The thought currents of passivity (Verse 14-8) make a direct assault on the consciousness through indolence, and perverted use of intelligence.

(4) The fourth variable of the suggested analytical framework is human ego. We have noted earlier that ego (E) is a byproduct of the union of the innate qualities of the Self and the body. As such ego is composed of two distinct parts. The first part, being the epitome of the Self, called (Verse 3-27) 'natural ego'. The natural ego, like the Self, is everlasting. It channels the inputs provided by the Self to every component of the domain of activity through the stream of active consciousness. The second part of human ego is called 'acquired ego'. It proxies the attributes of entities other than the Self. These entities, unlike the Self, are devoid of consciousness. The human instincts urge the acquired ego to gratify the senses, through attachment to the entities existing inside and or outside the domain. As a result ego functions as the agent of conscious activity. The tendency of acquired ego to be inclined towards the bodily and worldly concerns overshadows, but does not impair, the existence of natural ego. This is for reason of self-existent nature of natural ego. On the contrary, an impairment of acquired ego fosters natural ego. The natural ego creates an altogether different perspective for the working of the instruments (Chapter IV-5) of activity. The attributes of ego empower it to acclimatize itself either to the thought currents of passion or purity. The adaptation of ego to the propensity to passion causes the psychonomic perspective to be completely involved in the bodily and worldly concerns. On the other hand, the adaptation of ego to the propensity to purity enables the psychonomic perspective to capitalize on the innate attributes of the Self.

II-V THE VARIABLES RECONSIDERED

Thus far we have considered the relevance of the concept of micro order, specified its variables and noted the place of each in the strongly ordered domain of activity. But the preceding sections do not reveal the rationale of this elaborate exercise. Now we point out the rationale of our investigation. To this end, we consider the nature of variables comprising the micro order and their interaction with the entities existing outside oneself. The Self is the only entity endowed with consciousness. And all the entities other than the Self are devoid of consciousness. As such, the Self and entities other than the Self are respectively labeled as the 'alive' and 'non-alive' entities. The alive entity carries awareness of own self and all entities other than oneself. The non-alive entities are neither aware of their own existence, nor about the existence of any other entity. Further, we distinguish between the non-alive entities existing inside the domain and outside it. The non-alive entities obtaining inside the domain are in essence 'pseudo-alive' entities. This is for the reason that the alive entity (the Self) unceasingly infuses life energy, consciousness and intellectual light in these entities. The pseudo-alive entities constitute the domain of activity. The treatment of various entities opens an altogether fresh view about the concept of human capital. The Self, as a self-existent entity and the pseudo-alive entities comprising the micro order are respectively designated as the 'primary' and 'secondary' human capital. One notion of human capital without the other is a misnomer of human existence. The inputs (endowments) provided by the Supreme-Self through the Self and inputs provided by the nature through the pseudo-alive entities define the essence of the concept of human capital. The non-alive entities existing outside oneself are genuinely lifeless. They lack the awareness of own self as well as other entities. It is alleged that the Self (Verse 15-7 & 15-9) engages the five senses and the mind to enjoy non-alive entities through the objects of sense. We break up the passage of the alive to non-alive entities in four steps, namely, (1) from the alive to pseudo-alive entities, (2) from the pseudo-alive to the non-alive entities, (3) the non-alive entities react back on the pseudo-alive entities and (4) the pseudo-alive entities backfire on the alive entity. Each of these steps separately and together determines the psychonomic perspective obtaining in the micro order.

In the first step, the alive entity (the Self) steeps the non-alive entities inside the domain with life energy, knowledge and consciousness.

As a result the non-alive entities existing inside the domain become pseudo-alive entities. Each of these entities are stirred into action like the various parts of a machine. Each pseudo-alive entity carries out its own function, as decreed by nature, whose manifest form is the thought and effort contents of activity.

In the second step, the tail end of the pseudo-alive entities, namely, the senses are like causeway between the pseudo-alive entities, existing inside the domain, and non-alive entities existing outside the domain. In essence the outward projecting nature of the senses enables them to act as tools of perception and as a device to collect information about the non-alive entities existing outside the domain of activity. The subjective valuation of the non-alive entities by the internal instruments of activity discerns the utility of the entities perceived by the senses. The ever changing subjective valuation of the non-alive entities is constantly plotted on the preference map of individuals. The subjective valuation constitutes the axis (Chapter VI-2) which crowds out attachment towards the non-alive entities, as well as crowds attachment inside the domain of activity.

In the third step, the non-alive entities, obtaining outside the domain, being devoid of consciousness, create illusion of attraction and repulsion. In fact, the non-alive entities recoil the intensity of one's likes and dislikes as affixed by their subjective valuation by the internal instruments of activity. The non-alive entities like a mirror reflect the facts endorsed by the pseudo-alive entities. Consequently, the pseudo-alive entities are overrun by the impulses of attachment and aversion.

The fourth step, demonstrates the reaction of the pseudo-alive entities on the Self. The attachment to the non-alive entities incites likeability and pleasure. The obverse of attachment, aversion, gives rise to distaste, displeasure and pain. The pleasure or pain is staged by the pseudo-alive entities through self-indulgence. But the incidence of self-indulgence is born by the alive entity—the Self. The non-alive entities, existing either inside or outside the domain, are devoid of consciousness. As a result, they are in cable of causing the experience of pleasure or pain. The Self is thus reduced to be a courier of all the imperfections thrown up by the ever changing domain of activity.

This justifies our attempt to reconsider the variables of the suggested micro order. The supreme entity, the Self, frequently and helplessly bears the psychic-swings forced upon in (Verse 13-20) by the pseudo-alive entities. We view happiness and unhappiness as both as deviations impairing the welfare of individuals. Therefore, we go in search of the entity(ies) which disturb (Chapter V & VI) the spontaneous working of the micro order. The micro order if completely freed from the disturbances would certainly (Verse 18-45) conclude in a stable psychonomic perspective—the essence of human life. The Self despite being the seat of consciousness is inactive. It does not disturb the working of micro order. The same is true of the non-alive entities existing outside of oneself. They are essentially devoid of consciousness. The pseudo-alive entities must be the cause of unstable psychonomic perspective. This is for the reason that are in substance an assemblage of instruments of activity. But the user of the instrument, not the instrument, is accountable for the non-neutral working of the micro order. Our study affirms (Chapter IV, V, & VI) that human ego adapted to the thought currents of passion, at the instance of an individual's decision, upsets the natural working of the micro order. The cause of impairment of welfare of man is man himself.

*   *   *

CHAPTER-III

THE NATURE BORN TRIAD OF PROPENSITIES

The soul, nature, and the nature born triad of propensities are beginning less. The propensity to passion and passivity respectively activate action and deactivate action. The propensity to purity illuminates both kinds of activities and their outcome. The triads, to be brief, control all actions and change both at the level of cosmos and individuals. The Self, not the triad, set up relation of concern with the triad. The same is equally competent to relinquish the said relations. The playing field of the triad is the domain of activity through the stream of active consciousness. This approach helps us to establish (Chapter-III-1) the tie between the attributes of each propensity and the thought currents generated by them. The next issue of our concern (Chapter-III-2) is to explain the disparity between the thought currents of the triad of propensities. The impulse of attachment, born of the propensity to passion, is singled out as a factor which causes dissimilarly among the propensities. What matters most is the intensity of attachment. An increase in the intensity, drawn to an extreme invokes passivity. On the other hand, a decrease in attachment, again drawn to an extreme, transmutes the propensity to passion into purity. These arguments set the stage to consider the modus operandi of adjustments between the thought currents of the three propensities. The text postulates that the advance of one propensity is associated with the retreat of the other two propensities. The advance of a particular propensity (Chapter-III-3) is viewed as an issue in decision making. The decision to use the available means for one own self triggers the advance of the thought currents of passion. At the other end, the decision to devote the available means for the benefit of others sets off the thought currents of purity. The next section (Chapter-III-4) explains how the advance of the thought currents of passion is sustained and the same causes a retreat of the thought currents of the other two propensities. Finally, we consider (Chapter-III-5) how the advance of the thought currents of purity is sustained and the same induces a backward movement of the thought currents of passion and passivity. The advance of the thought current of a propensity implies that it occupies the upper segment of the stream of active consciousness, leaving the middle and the lower segments of the stream for the other two propensities.

III-1 SPECIFICATION OF THE TRIAD OF PROPENSITIES

The existence of individuals comprises the domain of activity (body) and the dweller in the domain—called the Self. The Self is beginning less and out of reach of the triad of propensities. For that reason, the Self despite being contained in the body (Verse 13-31 & 13-32) neither acts nor concerned with the activities carried out in the domain. It is alleged that there is no entity in the cosmos, including all beings, that is not the creation of the triad of propensities and free from (Verse 18-40) its attributes. In other words, the triad of propensities propels activities in an aggregate sense in the universe and also at the level of individuals as well. It implies that the instruments contained in the domain of activity, their functioning, the thought and effort contents of activity (Verse 5-9) and the personal nature of individuals (Verse 3-33) is the creation of the three propensities born of nature. Action signifies change. All activities embodying change occur in nature. Nature is intrinsically beset with change. And the Self is changelessness personified. The nature seldom becomes inactive and the Self rarely becomes active. These results set the stage for considering the general and specific nature of the triad of propensities.

In the first place, the extremely subtle nature of the propensities defies any description. The propensities are unobservable entities. But they are identifiable through their own creation of highly specific nature of the thought currents. The thought currents are less subtle as compared to the triad of propensities. The density of thought currents is heavier than the propensities of their origin. Consequently, the instruments of activity discern a propensity through the thought current generated by it. Secondly, the thought currents of each propensity rise and fall in the stream of active consciousness. Every one experiences and is aware of the changeable nature of the thought currents. It implies that there must be an entity which makes us aware of the changing nature of the thought currents. The Self through its attributes of changelessness (Chapter II-3) and endowed with consciousness helps to keep an eye on change. The viewer is not a part of the view. Thirdly, the Self being a self-existent entity (Verse 14-5) sets up relations of concern with the triad of propensities. The propensities lack the capacity to make, or unmake, the relation of concern with the Self. The Self enables awareness of the ever changing thought currents of the propensities. Therefore, neither the relation of concern built by the Self with the propensities, nor the propensities disturb the natural functioning of the micro order. In fact, every thought current originates (Verse 7-12) in the Self, but the self does not embody the thought currents, nor the thought currents contain the self. The triad of propensities are that of passion, passivity and purity.

The attribute of each propensity generates a specific set of thought currents. The description of the attributes and corresponding thought currents of each propensity is brought out as follows: (i) The propensity to passion (Verse 14-7) is attachment personified. The likable and engaging inclinations towards an object, person, event, circumstance and action are the manifestations of attraction closing in attachment. The propensity to passion triggers off action through the thought currents generated by it. The propensity animates (Verse 14-12) the thought currents of passion and, instinctive needs on the demand side and the urge to action—the mainspring of supply. The thought currents operative on the demand and supply sides act upon each other to actualize human activity. The third thought currents generated by the propensity to passion is greed—the urge for securing more than is right and reasonable. The motivator behind the thought currents of need, action and greed is the impulse of attachment in varying degrees. The first notable point is that the urge to action may, or may not, incorporate (Verse 14-7) the impulse of attachment. The urge to action could be attachment embodied, or attachment disembodied. This axiom is regardless of the fact that the urge to action and the impulse of attachment both originate in the propensity to passion. They are independent variables. In the second place, it follows that attachment embodied indulgence or abstaining from action both in effect are indulgence in action. The act of indulgence is (Verse 4-16) indicative of one facet of action and abstaining from action denotes another facet of action. Accordingly, the attachment disembodied indulgence or abstaining from action signifies delivery from the urge to action.

(2) The propensity to passivity personifies ignorance. It is alleged that although the propensity is born of ignorance (Verse 14-8), the same subsists upon ignorance. It implies that the propensity to passivity and ignorance are the cause and consequence of each other. The two reinforce and enhance each other. As a result the propensity deludes all living beings. It weakens the faculty to discern the difference between the self-existent and non-existent entities, duty and non-duty etc. The thought currents of 'negligence' and 'delusion' generated by the propensity to passivity sustain ignorance and thoughtlessness. The thought currents of negligence (Verse 14-13) cause one to become uncaring and inattentive about what should be done and not done. For this reason one tends to indulge in activities which impair the welfare of oneself and others both in the present and future. It also causes one to abstain from work which contributes to welfare. These tendencies are indicative of thoughtlessness as occasioned by passivity. The thought currents of negligence eclipse the brightness of wisdom in intelligence. One grows dimwitted and unimaginative, hence indifferent (Verse 18-39) to the consequences of one's own actions. The perspective of lethargy and sluggishness deactivate action. This is precisely the opposite of impact of the propensity to passion which activates the urge to action. An increase in the incidence of passivity evokes anti-wisdom tendencies by intensifying delusion. One is impelled, as if by force, to earn and amass wealth through unfair means and induced to incur wasteful expenditure. The propensity to passivity concentrates attention solely on one's own bodily concerns, which breeds arrogance, excessive pride and exaggerated notion of the self-sense of one's individuality.

(3) The propensity to purity, like the other two propensities is also nature born. But the propensity to purity remains absolutely untainted by the spillover effects produced by its thought currents. The propensities to passion and passivity, depending upon the intensity of attachment, are influenced in varying degrees by their own creation—that is, attachment-embodied thought contents of activity. The propensities to passion and passivity respectively subsist upon their own concocted selfish-will and ignorance. But the propensity to purity is marked by complete non-appearance of the level of attachment in excess of that is decreed to fulfill the will of nature. The will of nature signifies spontaneous (Verse 18-45) working of the micro order, unpolluted by

the motives inducing attachment to self-indulgence and accumulation of wealth. The impulse of attachment, un-aggravated by selfishness and motive fixed in gratification of the senses, escalates the assimilation of the qualities of the Self in the domain through the intelligence. The propensity to purity generates the thought currents of 'illumination' and 'knowledge'. The thought currents of illumination brighten the incidence of insight and foresight in intelligence. For this reason, a disposition of ego-lessness thoroughly cleanses the intelligence and mind (Verse 14-11) of the imperfections and flaws caused by the propensities of passion and passivity. One can clearly visualize wholly unconstrained by the rise and fall of the thought currents of passion and passivity. As a result, the instruments of perception and action cease to be prejudiced by attachment and aversion. Now the self-sustaining zeal to action makes the optimal use of intelligence possible, unrestrained by any manifestation of attachment. It is relevant to note (Verse 7-11) that the zeal and enthusiasm impelled by selfish desires and attachment do not give rise to self-sustained impetus to work. The thought currents of knowledge born of purity enable one to clearly distinguish between what is to be accepted and rejected, duty and non-duty, that is self-existent and non-existent and between change and changelessness. The psychonomic perspective rising above the bondage of work adapted to satisfy selfish desires, experiences (Verse 18-37) delight in intelligence. It implies that short-run bliss imparted by sensual pleasures gives way to lasting ecstasy and contentment.

For this reason the propensity in its purest form (Verse 14-6) establishes the control on the animator of the domain of activity (or the Self) over the domain of activity. In other words, the exploitation of the endowments of the Self and nature foster each other to attain supreme (Verse 3-12) welfare. It naturally follows that the propensity to purity in a mixed form—that is, tainted by the urge to gratify the senses, adjusts the psychonomic perspective to indulge in discoveries, inventions and innovations, but does not conclude the attainment of welfare—enduring peace, happiness for oneself and others.

III-2 THE CAUSE OF DISPARITY AMONG THE THOUGHT CURRENTS OF THE TRIAD OF PROPENSITIES.

The preceding section has explained the correspondence between the attributes and the thought currents of the triad of propensities. Before we consider the mode of interaction (Chapter III-3) between the thought currents of propensities, one issue has to be resolved. The issue to be settled is what makes the thought currents of the three propensities to be so different. The stream of active consciousness, supposedly originating from the Self, must in essence be absolutely clean and clear. The stream is flawless, pure, distinct and comprehensible. But the propensities to passion and passivity taint the stream of active consciousness, for reason of their qualitatively different attributes. But it is easy to identify the factor which, so to say, coats the thought currents of the propensities with different colors. The causative facts born of the propensity to passion, is the impulse of attachment. The propensity to passion, being primarily driven by instincts outstrips the other two propensities. As a result, the impact of the impulse of attachment spreads over a much wider canvas, that to with varying intensity. The length and breadth of the canvas and the cause which determines the intensity is considered (Chapter-V) subsequently. At this stage, we demonstrate how the varying intensity of attachment concocts different attributes of the thought currents of propensities. The impulse of attachment overtakes perception by the senses, thinking sequence by the mind and decision making by the intelligence. We conjecture and ordinal scale to measure the intensity of attachment between zero to one. The middle portion of the scale denotes the display of a moderate intensity of attachment. The placement of the moderate intensity in the middle portion signifies that (I) the rightward movement along the scale cause the intensity to tend to one, and (II) the leftward movement along the scale, causes the intensity of attachment tend to zero. We contend that as the intensity of attachment tends to one, the propensity to passion is transformed into passivity. In the same way, as the intensity of attachment tends to zero, the propensity to passion gives way to purity. The change in the form and substance of one into another propensity comes into being through discrete steps. It is closely associated with (Chapter-V) qualitative change in the thought content of activity. To illustrate, selfish motive signifies passivity and passion, and unselfish motive signifies purity.

However, at this stage we propose to consider the impact of varying intensity of attachment of the nature of propensities. It is premised that the intensity of attachment affects the nature of propensities through its impact on the quality of thought contents engendered by a propensity. The density of the thought contents is an indicator of the quality of thought contents of activity. The term density refers to the psychic burden or heaviness associated with a given thought content. It is alleged that (Verse 14-11) the thought currents of purity are lighter, or less heavy, or less burdensome, or less oppressive than the thought currents of the other two propensities. For this reason, we contend that while the thought contents of purity are attachment-disembodied, the thought contents of the other two propensities are attachment-embodied. This inference follows the fact that (Verse 14-7) the propensity to passion is an embodiment of attachment. It is observed that an increase (decrease) in the density of thought content is associated with and increase (decrease) in the intensity of attachment. But an increase (decrease) in the intensity of attachment is attended by a decrease (increase) in the brightness of wisdom in intelligence. The wisdom can be eclipsed not erased by attachment as wisdom, like the Self, is self-existent and (Verse 18-16) attachment is transient in nature. The logic presented above helps to draw the following results. In the first place, an increase in the intensity of attachment retards the incidence of wisdom in intelligence and increases the density of thought contents of activity. For this reason, as one moves from the middle portion of the conjectured, ordinal scale of attachment to the right, the thought currents of (i) passion merge into the thought currents of passivity. It implies that (ii) an advance of the propensity to passion or passivity would cause a retreat of the propensity to purity in the stream of active consciousness. Secondly, a decrease in the intensity of attachment increases the incidence of wisdom in intelligence and decreases the density of thought contents of activity. Consequently, as one moves from the middle portion of the ordinal scale of attachment to the left (i) the thought currents of passion merge into the thought currents of purity. It means that (ii) the propensity to purity becomes the leading propensity causing a retreat of the other two propensities. These results are of immense significance for the logical basis of the arguments ahead.

III-3 MODUS OPERANDI OF THE THOUGHT CURRENTS OF THE TRIAD.

The text provides us with two postulates to consider the dynamic adjustment between the thought currents of the three propensities. The first postulate states (Verse 14-10) that the propensity to purity moves forward by pushing back the propensities to passion and passivity. The propensity to passion moves forward by driving back the propensities to purity and passivity. In the same manner, the propensity to passivity moves forward by pushing the propensities of passion and purity backward. In other words, the advance of the thought currents of a given propensity is coupled with a retreat of the thought currents of the other two propensities. The second postulate (Versa 14-18) makes a note on the relative strength of propensities which contribute to the growth, stationeries and impairment of human welfare.

We begin with the first postulate first. The dynamic adjustment between the three propensities raises the following issues to be resolved. The issues are (1) why a particular propensity begins to move forwards. What sustains (2) its forward movement? How the advance (3) of a propensity brings about a retreat of the other two propensities. The second and the third issue are treated (Chapter III-4 & III-5) subsequently. The answer to the first issue is that the decision of an individual causes a particular propensity to make an advance. The logical basis of decision making encircles the proportion in which the available means is divided to be used for one's own welfare and the welfare of others. We assume that each individual is concerned with wishes and needs of own self as well as with the needs and wishes of others. The decision problem crops up when once has to decide whether the concern for oneself is greater, equal to, or less than the consideration for others. It is premised that the decision adapted to selfish desires and self-serving work triggers the thought currents of passion more than the thought currents of the other two propensities. The means available to an individual denotes the totality of received inputs from nature or the domain of activity, the Self and macro order. The macro order supports individuals till their demise, installs skill, helps to exploit talent and makes all kinds of inputs and non-human capital available within their reach.

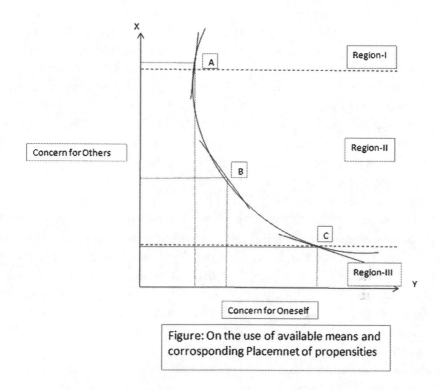

Figure: On the use of available means and corrosponding Placemnet of propensities

Given the total amount of received inputs, an increase (decrease) in the concern for one self, would entail decrease (increase) in the concern for others. Let the X an Y axes, in a two dimensional presentation, respectively measure the extent of concern for one self and concern for other selves. Any point on the down sloping curve of concern, drawn between the two axes, reflects varying combination of the said concern. A downward movement along the curve increasingly increases the concern for one self, discrediting the concern for others. Similarly, an upward movement along the curve increasingly increases the concern for others, but decreasing concern for one self. Let the budget line, as used in indifference curve analyses, denote the total means available to and individual. It is suggested that an individual is free to choose any point of tangency between the budget line and the down sloping curve of concern. The point of tangency, each point of tangency, is an indicator of the choice of a "particular individual" for an optimal combination of concern for one self and other selves. It implies that three different individuals can be situate at the points of tangency indicated by A, B and C. It is also implies that an individual can give up one optimal combination of concern and choose another overtime. We also conduct another experiment to get more results. Let the two dimensional space be divided into three regions to focus upon the relative incidence of the thought currents of each propensity. This is done to work out the implications of the second postulate. We contend that the placement of thought currents of the three propensities in the stream of active consciousness depends upon the decision of an individual itself. The Region-II denotes the most generally observed incidence of the thought currents of the three propensities. The thought currents of passion, passivity and purity respectively occupy the upper, middle and lower segments of the stream of active consciousness. The location of the thought currents, in the said stream, keeps the welfare of an individual at a stationary level. This is for the reason that the optimal combinations of concern below, so also above the point B, within the Region-II reflect compensating concern for oneself and others. The ordinal measure of welfare remains unchanged because (a) the points below B indicate that an increasing concern for oneself is offset by decreasing concern for others. Similarly, the points above B indicate the (b) decreasing concern for oneself is offset by increasing concern for others. In contrast, all the selected optimal positions falling in the Region-III and Region-I respectively indicate loss or gain in welfare. Now we cannot escape to specify the test of welfare dealt (Chapter-VII) elsewhere. A tendency which causes the psychonomic perspective to be driven by the steady state of intelligence contributes to one's own welfare. Conversely, the tendency(ies) causing deviations from the steady state of intelligence impair one's own welfare. The move towards the optimal points of concern, falling in the Region-III, indicate increasingly increasing disregard for the concern of others. This tendency breeds conflicts, care, anxiety and degenerates into manifestation of aversion and violence. The loss of welfare grows proportional to the increasing concern for oneself. On the other hand, the Region-I presents precisely an opposite situation. The gain on one's own welfare increasingly increases till (Chapter-VII-4) one is established in the steady state of intelligence. The increasingly increasing concern for others (Verse 3-11) is suggested to be used as a tool to enhance one's own welfare. The Region-I may, however, register two (Verse 14-6) categories of optimal concerns. In the first category the thought currents of passion take a lead and the thought currents of purity run parallel to it. In the second category of optimal concerns the thought currents of purity, passion and passivity respectively appear in the upper, middle and lower segments of the stream of active consciousness.

Thus it is concluded that the use of available means, or the total inputs provided by one's body, the Self (soul) and the macro order to enhance one's own welfare sets off the thought currents of passion, followed by the thought currents of passivity and purity. As against this, the decision to use the available means to enhance the welfare of others causes an advance of the thought currents of passion, with almost a parallel move of the thought currents of purity, followed by the thought currents of passivity.

III-4 THE FORWARD MOVEMENT OF THE THOUGHT CURRENTS OF PASSION

The preceding section has dealt at length how the decision to use the available means may either cause the thought currents of passion or purity to move forward. The two remaining issues regarding the dynamic adjustment of the three propensities are (1) what sustains the advance of the leading propensity and (2) how the leading propensity causes the thought currents of the other two propensities to move backwards. Now we assume that the passion is the leading propensity. The use of available means (Chapter-III-4) to enhance one's own welfare provokes the thought currents of passion to move forward. The thought currents of passion, passivity and purity respectively occupy the upper, middle and lower segments of the stream of active consciousness.

The forward movement of the thought currents of passion is sustained by three separate reasons. In the first place, the passion driven self indulgence (Verse 18-38) fixes one's motive in pleasure seeking. The said motive is instinctive. The urge to self-indulgence is effortless and spontaneous, hence provokes the advance of the thought currents of passion. The reaction in terms of pleasure to an agreeable context, so also displeasure in disagreeable context is noticeable since birth. Secondly, the urge to neediness and action, as the subsets of the thought currents of propensity to passion, sustain its advance. The tendency of the two subsets of thought currents to strengthen each other is escalated by the impulse of greed, also born of the propensity to passion. Thirdly, although the propensity to passion is nature born, yet its thought currents make an advance because passion subsists on its own generated thought contents of activity. The passion and passion driven thoughts are the cause (Verse 14-7) and consequence (Verse 3-37) of each other. The cause and consequence interacting upon each other sustain the forward movement of the thought currents of passion.

The dynamic adjustment (Verse 14-10) also occasions the leading propensity to be associated with a retreat of the other two propensities. The forward movement of the propensity to passion results in a retreat of the thought currents of passivity and purity. The rise of passion aggravates the impulses of attachment as well as the urge to activity. An increase in both these impulses tones down the thought currents of passivity and purity for two reasons. In the first place, while the intensification of attachment (Chapter-III-3) overshadows the brightness of wisdom in intelligence. The same excites rise of the prevailing thought currents of passivity in other words, while an increase in the intensity of attachment discourages the thought currents of purity, the same encourages the thought currents of passivity through ignorance. Secondly, the intensification of the urge to activity discourages negligence and delusion of passivity. But the escalation of passion impels purity to embody attachment, hence further cast down purity. The joint impact of the intensification of attachment and urge to activity is to push the thought currents of purity to retreat. On the other hand, the thought currents of passivity are encouraged by intensification of attachment, but discouraged by activation of the urge to action. The net effect on the thought currents of passivity is to move backwards. This is for the reason that the urge to action itself begins to be impelled by attachment. Thus the forceful advance of the urge to activity retards the thought currents of passivity.

It is also noticeable that the retreat of the thought currents of the propensities of passivity and purity reinforce each other, to make the advance of passion possible. This is for the reason that the weakened thought currents of purity amplify passivity by encouraging negligence and delusion. The obtaining tendencies of passivity tend to darken illumination of purity.

III-5 THE FORWARD MOVEMENT OF THE THOUGHT CURRENT OF PURITY

Now we assume purity to be the leading propensity. It implies that the available means (Chapter-III-4) is used for the benefit of others, keeping due regard for one's own needs and wishes. Thus the thought currents of passion, purity and passivity respectively occupy the upper, middle and lower segments of the stream of active consciousness. The issues which engage attention now are (a) what sustains the advance of the thought currents of purity and (b) how the thought currents of purity are associated with the retreat of the thought currents of the other two propensities.

The advance of the thought currents of purity is sustained because of two reasons. In the first place, an interaction between the subsets of thought currents of purity, namely illumination and knowledge, foster each other to ease the advance of purity. The two subsets respectively correspond to the flow and stock aspects of the propensity to purity. The thought currents of illumination enlighten perception and decisions making as purified by the onset of wisdom in intelligence. Thus the flow aspect of the thought currents constantly add to the stock aspect, that is the thought currents of knowledge. The thought currents of knowledge as a repository ensure regular supply of pure perception and decision. The net impact of illumination and knowledge is to enhance the concern for the welfare of others, sustaining the spirit of sacrifice. Such a radical change in attitude activates yet another cause to keep the advance of the thought currents of purity going. It is the weakening of the incidence of acquired ego on the domain of activity. Consequently, intelligence is enabled to assimilate the intrinsic qualities of the Self. This phenomenon sets in delight in intelligence, (Verse 14-10). It is caused by the enhanced influence of the Self, through the natural ego, on the intelligence.

The dynamic adjustment (Verse 14-10) also causes the leading propensity to induce a retreat of the thought currents of the other two propensities. The forward move of the thought currents of purity result in a retreat of the thought currents of passion and passivity. The thought currents of purity engender retreat through two different routes. The two routes are curtailment of the intensity of attachment and intensification of the impact of wisdom in intelligence. It is noticeable that both these routes reinforce the advance of each other. A decrease in the intensity of attachment increases the impact of wisdom and the increased brightness of wisdom discourages the tendency of attachment to prevail. Let us consider the first route first. The advance of the thought currents of purity highlights the end result (Verse 18-36) of each thought and action content of activity. The transient considerations give way to the search for something enduring. It implies that the thought currents of purity cause to one to turn away from self-indulgence and accumulation of wealth to satisfy one's ego. This is a consequence of weakening of acquired ego as it growingly adapts to the thought currents of purity. The ebb of passion in acquired ego spontaneously increases the incidence of purity on natural ego. The rise of natural ego effectively channels the qualities of the Self into the instruments of activity through the intelligence. The instruments of activity are cleansed off the thought currents of passion and passivity. The micro order is thoroughly stripped off the impulses of attachment, greed, negligence and the delusion simulated by passivity. It is noticeable that an increase in the attachment—disembodied urge to activity itself accelerates the retreat of the incidence of passivity on the domain of activity. And the retreat of passivity in turn paves the way for the advance of the pure urge to activity.

The conclusions presented in Chapter-III-4 and Chapter-III-5 provide the basis for further reasoning dealt in Chapter-IV-4, Chapter-V and Chapter-VI. The results of Chapter-III-4 and Chapter-III-6 provide the raw material to develop the arguments presented in Chapter-VII.

*   *   *

CHAPTER-IV

WORKING OF THE STYLIZED MODEL OF THE MICRO ORDER

It is premised that working of the suggested micro order is controlled by an interaction between the four variables, namely, the Self, instruments of activity, triad of propensities and human ego. We assert that (Chapter-IV-1) that each variable influences the other three variables and is in turn influenced by them. The logic of each variable dependent upon other variables yields a set of twelve relationships among four variables. The search for general interdependence, in the context of twelve relationships would be highly complicated. Therefore, we re-specify the rationale of the working of (Chapter IV-2) micro order. We find that the direction of change in the operation of the variables depends upon a change in the composition of ego, followed by a corresponding change in the mix of the thought currents of the three propensities. This finding explains the substance of working of the micro order. This rationale of the working of the suggested order led us to consider (Chapter-IV-4) the ego-embodied model of micro order. The adaptation of ego to the thought currents of the propensity to passion makes for the ego-embodied model. The ego arbitrates between the Self and domain of activity to establish an order based of the fulfillment of selfish desires. The key concern is one own self. The final section (Chapter-IV-5) assumes the ego to be adapted to the thought currents of the propensity to purity. This exercise gives rise to the egoless model of micro order. The primary concern of this model is welfare of others, without disregarding one's own needs and wishes.

IV-1 THE BASIS OF INTERACTION AMONG THEVARIABLES

The working of the model of micro order is postulated to depend upon an interaction among the variables constituting the order. The variables are the Self(S), triad of propensities (T), ego(E) and instruments of activity(I). Now we go in search of the basis to scan the interdependence among variables. Let us take a resort to the following expository device.

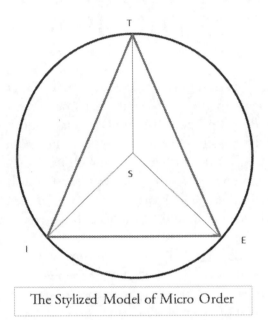

The Stylized Model of Micro Order

The three corners of the triangle TEI respectively depict the location of the variables (T), (E) and (I). The variable (S) occupies the centre of the triangle TEI. The straight lines radiating from the center connect the three corners of the triangle TEI. Thus we have three straight lines inside and three straight lines outside defining the boundary of TEI. Now we can probe onto the mode of interaction among the variables obtaining at the end of each straight lines this exercise yields two significant results to specify the nature of interdependence among the variables. In the first place, each straight line carries a variable at its both ends. The straight line exhibits the effect of two variables on each other. Thus six straight lines are indicative of twelve relationships among four variables. The effect of a variable on the other could be equal to, more or less than the effect of the other on the former variable. The two variables act and react upon each other to weaken or strengthen the other variable. Secondly, each of the three corners, so also the centre of the triangle TEI, emit three straight lines to reach other variables, to illustrate, the straight lines emitted by the variable (I) connect it to the variables (E), (T) and (S). It implies that each variable influences the other three variables and is also influenced by them in turn.

The set of twelve relationships provide us with a complete view of general interdependence among four variables. But it is highly complicated to delve into twelve relationships to ascertain the working of micro order. Therefore, the methodical elegance required us to reconsider the issue. Now each of the six straight lines describe the action and reaction between two variables only. The resulting twelve relationships among the four variables can be reduced to six net effects. The notion of net effect signifies that the influence of one on the other variable could be the same, more or less than the influence of the other. In other words, the give-and-take relation between the two variables may cause the value of net effect to be equal to zero, positive or negative. The positive net effect implies that the effect of the first on the second variable is greater than the effect of the second on the first variable. Similarly, the net effect with a negative sign implies that the influence of the first on the second variable is stronger than the influence of the second on the first. The net effect, in substance does not bring to bear any influence on variables other than those at the two ends of a given straight line. It means that the impact of each net effect on the remaining two variables would help deduce lessons regarding the general interdependence among the four variables of the micro order.

The suggested expository device is intended to place all the four variables in the context of general equilibrium. It comprises six net effects, namely (TI), (TE), (EI), (ES) and (IS). But the notion of net effect expresses the cross influence between two variables only. It implies that the notion of net effect exhibits (i) the reciprocal relation only between the two variables included in a given net effect, hence (ii) does not explain the changes in the other two variables not included in a given net effect. It implies that each net effect must account for its influence upon the variables not included in that net effect. To illustrate, the net effect (TE) explains the influence of the variable (T) on (E), which may be equal or unequal to the influence of the variable (E) on (T). Further, it is suggested that the net effect (TE) also considers the impact of its combined influence on the variables (S) and (I). In other words, (TE) »

I and (TE) » S would place each net effect (TE) in the context of general equilibrium. But the conduct of this exercise in case of the remaining five net effects would yield ten more results. Once again the analysis would become unmanageable.

IV-2 THE BASIS OF INTERDEPENDENCE REVISITED

The rationale of the working of the micro order requires us to identify the key determinant of the state of the order. It can be shown that none of the four variables all by themselves can be the key factor to explain the changing state of the micro order. In the first place, the Self(S) is an epitome of inactive consciousness. Secondly, the functioning of the variable (I) depends upon the inputs infused by the Self. Further, the instruments (I) contained in the body without the Self and the Self without the body can neither carry out and activities, nor accommodate any action. Thirdly, the variable (T) fixes the direction in which the instruments contained in the body functions. But the role of the variable (T) depends upon the Self. The relation of concern set up by the Self activates the thought currents of propensities in the domain of activity. Finally, the very existence of the variable (E) depends upon the union of the Self and the body devised by the variable (T). Consequently, it appears that there must be some key net effect which controls the state of micro order. In fact, the decision of an individual regarding the use of available means (Chapter-III-3) makes for the key net effect. Therefore, we conclude that a net effect vitalized by an individual's decision must be the mainspring of the changes in the state of micro order.

Now we go in search of the key net effect. It acts as the mainspring of the changes in the micro order. We have pointed out earlier two issues to be resolved for demonstrating the dependence of each variable on the other variables. In the first place, each of the six net effects must account for its impact on the two variables not included in it. Secondly, the combined impact of each net effect on the variables not included in the net effect is explicitly shown to complete the analysis. This approach, to repeat, is intended to uncover the general interdependence among the four variables of the micro order. Now we propose to deal separately the net effect (IS). This is for the reason, the net effect (IS) is a complete representation of the micro order, as the symbol (S) and (I) respectively denote the Self and the instruments contained in the domain of activity.

This line of reasoning requires the specification of the rein remaining five net effects, along with the variables not included in each net effect. Thus we have following functions:

(S) «(TE) »(I)
(E) «(TI)» (S)
(E)»(TS)» (I)
(T) «(ES) »(I)
(T)» (EI) »(S)

A close scrutiny of the above representation yields a few significant conclusions. In the first place, the net effect (TE) is the only one which can be accepted as the key net effect. This is for the reason that, any change in the variable T and/or the variable E affects the entire micro order—that is, both the Self (S) and the instruments (I) contained in the domain of activity. Secondly, we also observe that any change in the variables (T) and/or (E) affects the remaining net effects in one way or the other. Thirdly, it is also noticeable that the net effect (TI), so also the net effect (EI), influences the variable the Self (S). It is submitted the nature of change in the Propensity-mix(P-mix) and Ego-mix(E-mix) determine the favorable or unfavorable impact on the Self. Finally, the net effect (TS), so also the net effect (ES), influence the composition of received input-mix by the variable (I). The following two sections (Chapter IV-3) and (Chapter III-4) would seek an answer to the following four issues. To recapitulate (1) how the key net effect (TE) directly affects the variables (S) and (I). The key net effect (2) influences the variables (S) and (I) indirectly through changes in composition of Propensity-mix and Ego-mix. How the changes in the net effects (3) (TI) and (EI) influence the variable (S). How the net effects (TS) and (ES) influence the quality of (4) input-mix received by the variable (I).

IV-3 THE EGO-EMBODIED MODEL OF MICRO ORDER

It was shown earlier (Chapter III-3) that the decision to use the available means may be urged by the motive to improve one's own welfare. This decision simultaneously induces a change in the composition of ego and the thought currents of the triad of propensities. This is because the selfish motive impels one to maximize gains from others, their work and the outcome of work. The selfish motive strengthens acquired ego over natural ego. In other words, natural ego is eclipsed by the motive to gratify the senses. This tendency spontaneously causes the thought currents of passion to advance (Chapter III-3) enforcing a retreat of the thought currents of the other two propensities. The change in the composition of ego and the thought currents of the triad of propensities is reflected in simultaneous change in the, so to say, in the E-mix and P-mix. The urge to gratify the senses is actualized by the propensity to passion. This is for the reason that (Verse 14-7) the propensity to passion is an embodiment of attachment and the urge to gratify the senses activates the impulse of attachment. As a result, acquired ego and thought currents of passion reinforce and enhance each other. We conclude that consistent changes in the E-mix and P-mix intensify the impact of the key net effect (TE/ET=1). This is for the reason that ego as the shelter of (Verse 3-34) attachment and desire born (Verse 3-40) of selfish-will acclimatizes itself to the thought currents of passion. These arguments explain the essence of the ego-embodied model of micro order.

The analytical framework (Chapter IV) tells us that the key net effect (TE/ET = 1) directly affects the variable (S) and the variable (I). The thought currents of passion and ego together impel the use of the inputs provide by the Self, through the instruments contained in the domain of activity, to gratify the senses. This implies that the incidence of the impulse of attachment and the self-sense of one's individuality is intensified by selfish-will. To put it differently, the contributions of the variable (E) through acquired ego and of the variable (T) through the thought currents of passion to the input-mix of the variable (I) tend to be non-neutral. The inputs grow non-neutral when the thought content constituting the inputs sustain and magnify the negative thoughts originating from maximization of gains and minimization of losses for oneself. The underlying selfish-will tends to contain the impulse of attachment and the self-sense of individuality (Chapter VI-2) inside the domain of activity. The direct impact of the key net effect (TE/ET = 1) is to saturate the input-mix of the variable (I) with non-neutral inputs.

The key net effect (TE/ET = 1) also controls the input-mix of the variables (I) through the other net effects, namely, (TI), (TS), (EI) and (ES). Each of these net effects influence the variables not included in them. The sorting out of variables not included in the net effects (TI) and (TS) are the variables (E), (I) and (S). The same exercise for the variables not included in the net effects (ES) and (EI) are the variables (T), (I) and (S). The combined impact of the noted four net effects appears in three directions.

In the first place, all the four net effects reinforce the impact generated by the impact generated by the key net effect (TE/ET) = 1 on the input-mix of the variable (I). This conclusion follows from the effect that the net effects (TI) and (TS) influence the variable (E) and the net effects (EI and ES) influence the variable (T). These separate influences on the variables (T) and (E) intensify the impact of the key net effect (TE/ET = 1). The input-mix of the variable (I) gets permeated by the various manifestations of the impulse of attachment and egoism. Secondly, the variable (T) of the net effects (TI) and (TS), so also the variable (E) of the net effects (EI) and (ES) again foster precisely the same impact on the input-mix of the variable (I) as the key net effect. Consequently, every instrument contained in the domain of activity is precepted by the impulse of attachment and egoism. Thirdly, the net effects (TI) and (EI) both influence the variable (S) not included in them. The impact of these influences on the variable (S) also influences the input-mix of the variable (I). It is notable that the variable (S) being a self existent entity and beyond the reach of egoism and attachment unceasingly provides neutral inputs in the input-mix. The combined impact of the key and other net effects is to embody the input—mix of the variable (I) with non-neutral inputs, which negate the influence of the neutral inputs provides by the Self.

Now the function of the variable (I) acquires great significance. The variable (I), like a machine, receives its input-mix from the variables (S), (T), and (E) and transforms the input-mix into the output-mix. But the variable (I) remains unmindful about the quality of the received input-mix and the quality of the output-mix produced by it. We dwell for a while upon the ingredients comprising the input-mix. The variable (S) as a contributor to the input-mix ensures a guaranteed and unchanging supply of wisdom, insight and foresight into the domain of activity. These inputs are neutral in substance. This is for reason of their being untainted either by attachment or aversion. As against this, the pseudo-alive entities interacting with the non-alive entities generate the compelling force of attraction, causing attachment, and repulsion, causing aversion. The adaptation of the propensity to passion by acquired ego activates various manifestations of attachment in varying degrees in countless directions. This episode itself grows operative as an independent variable in the micro order. The impulse of attachment and its obverse aversion taints every thought content to become non-neutral. The constant supply of neutral inputs by the Self tends to be eclipsed by the non-neutral attributes of the thought content of activity. As a result the output-mix produced by the variable (I) contains a very high ratio of the non-neutral to the neutral thought contents of activity.

It is notable that the ratio of non-neutral to neutral thought contents of activity produced by the variable (I) affects significantly all the variables of the micro order—that is, the variables (S), (T), (E), as well as the variable (I) itself. The impact of the output-mix on the Self (S) is considered separately. The resulting output-mix fosters the reinforcing relation between the variables (T) and (E) instigated by the attachment embodied thought contents of activity. As a result the key net effect (TE/ET = 1) wields its inexorable impact on the micro order by involving other net effects as well. What is of utmost importance now is to examine the impact of output-mix on the working of every instrument contained in the domain of activity. The encroachment of attachment and aversion in every instrument of activity generates (Chapter VI-3) subjective constraints and gives rise to (Chapter VI-4) psychic swings in the psychonomic perspective. The end result is constrained human activity impairing the welfare of individuals. The partial to non-appearance of wisdom in intelligence breeds irrational thought contents closing in suboptimal use of the instruments of activity. The impetuous nature of the senses and mind seize the psychonomic perspective into the whirl of attachment and aversion. The unstable intelligence tends to conceal the influence of wisdom infused by the Self.

The working of the ego-embodied model gives rise to the following conclusions. We identify two compelling forces which discompose the working of the domain of activity whose spillover effect is borne by the Self. These compelling forces emerge from the key net effect (TE/ET = 1). The first binding force emanates from its entry into the net effects (TS) and (TI) influencing the variable (S). The second binding for force arises from the key net effect find finding its entry into the net effects (ES) and (EI) influencing the variable (I).

Let us consider the first binding force first. The key net effect (TE/ET = 1) finds its entry into the net effects (TS) and (ES) by generating the attachment embodied thought contents of activity. The attachment to all kinds of tangible and intangible objects, including one's own thought and body, renders the Self (S) helpless in percepting the use of its own inputs provided to the domain of activity. The Self despite being the only provider of unique inputs passively follows the decree of the user of these inputs. The user—that is, the domain, not the Self, sets the rules of the game. This is for the reason that the variable (T) through the thought currents of passion and the variable (E) through acquired ego cause the variables (T) and (E) to overshoot the influence of the variable (S) on (T) and (E).

Secondly, the strength of attachment-embodied thought contents of activity also instigate the urge to gratify the senses. Consequently, the Self upholds the incidence of ceaseless change of the entities existing outside the domain and its spillover impact on the entities existing inside the domain. This is for the reason that the variable (S), and embodiment of life energy and consciousness, animates the entities existing inside the domain of activity.

The key net effect (TE/ET = 1) also finds its entry into the net effects (TI) and (EI) to influence the Self. The Self is influenced by the output-mix produced by the variable (I). As a result the influence of the variable (I) on (T) and (E) is of the same strength as the influence of the variables (T) and (E) on (I). The variable (T) and (E) contribute non-neutral inputs to build the input-mix of the variable (I). The variable (I) transforms the received input-mix into the output of non-neutral contents of activity. The non-neutral thoughts arise from the desires born (Chapter V) of selfish-will and attachment to every aspect (Chapter VI) of work. The variables (S) grows defenseless, hence acts as the cause of experience of the bewildering influence of the non-neutral thought contents of activity. The Self the helplessness of the Self is not an outcome of cessation of injection of wisdom into the stream of active consciousness but due to the eclipse caused by the attachment-embodied thought contents of activity.

IV-4 THE EGOLESS MODEL OF MICRO ORDER

The analytical framework of the foregoing section can also be used to build the egoless model of micro order. The ego steps in relation between the Self and the instruments contained in the domain of activity. For this reason, the impact of the intensification of ego provided us with the ego-embodied model, and now it's damping down will yield the egoless model. Now we assume that ego acclimatizes it self to the thought currents of purity rather than the thought currents of passion. But ego simply carries out the decision made by an individual. One may decide (Chapter III-3) to use the available means for the welfare of others, without disregarding one's own. The substitution of the unselfish for selfish motive externalizes the impulse of attachment and egoism sustained by selfish-will, out of the domain. The urge to selfless service and the spirit of sacrifice actualizes the unselfish motive. It is contended that the radical change in decision, as before, simultaneously induces a consistent change in the E-mix and P-mix. A decrease in the urge to self-indulgence, because of selflessness produces a change in the composition of ego. The acquired ego ceases to ellipse the natural ego. The motive of selflessness delivers natural ego from the highly restrictive implications of self-centeredness. This is a deep-seated change in the E-mix. The sprit of selflessness, operating through natural ego, disconnects the urge to activity and the impulse of attachment. It is emphasized that (Verse 14-7) the urge to activity can be attachment-embodied or attachment-disembodied. This is a truism, despite the fact that the impulse of attachment and the urge to activity both originate in the propensity to passion. The spirit of self-denial and growing strength of natural ego foster each other to induce a retreat of the thought currents of passion and encourage the advance of the thought currents of purity. A decrease in the strength of passion and increase in the strength of purity set in a radical change in the P-mix. It is also notable that (i) a decrease in the strength of acquired ego, (ii) increase in the force of natural ego, (iii) abatement of the thought currents of passion and (iv) strengthening of the thought currents of purity escalate consistent changes in the E-mix and P-mix. In other words, the same directional changes in the variables (T) and (E) again establish (TE/ET = 1) as the key net effect. The net effect (TE/ET = 1) bears upon the entire micro order—that is, the on the variable (S) and instruments contained in the domain of activity.

The thought currents of purity and natural ego make the net effect key functional in the micro order. In three distinct Steps. The first and second steps show the direct and indirect impact of the net effect (TE/ET = 1) on the input-mix of the variable (I). The third step shows the impact of transformation of the received input-mix into the output-mix produced by the variable (I) on the variables (T) and (E) and on the variable (I) itself. The final step reveals the impact of resulting output-mix on the Self. Let us consider how the net effect (TE/ET = 1) directly acts upon the input-mix of the variable (I). In the first place, the thought currents of purity and natural ego enhance the effectiveness of the unceasing supply of neutral inputs by the Self to the instruments of activity. It may be added that the inputs become neutral when the thought contents embodied in them sustain the positive notions to improve the welfare of others. In other words, the impact of neutral inputs on every instrument of activity is fostered by the variables (T) and (E), both separately and together through the key net effect (TE/ET = 1). The net effect delivers the input-mix of the variable (I) from the repercussions of the impulses of attachment and self-centeredness. This is for the reason that attachment, egoism and selfish-will are expelled out of the domain to improve the welfare of others. The net effect (TE/ET = 1) infuses the variable (I) with neutral inputs, which do not undermine the contributions of the Self.

The key net effect (TE/ET = 1) also controls the input-mix indirectly through other net effects, namely, (TS), (TI), (ES) and (EI). Each of these net effects influence the variable (I) through their impact on the variables not included in them. The sorting out of the variables not included in these four net effects are the variables (T), (E), (I) and (S). The combined impact of the noted net effects can be discerned in three directions. In the first place, all the four net effects reinforce the impact generated by the key net effect on the input-mix of the variable (I). This for reason of radical changes in the E-mix and P-mix Which sustain and strengthen each other. Secondly, now the net effects (TS) and (TI) through the variable (T), and the net effects (ES) and (EI) through the variable (E) intensify the impact on the input-mix as created by the key net effect. Consequently, every instrument contained in the domain of activity is thoroughly cleansed of the impurities brought forth by the various manifestations of attachment, including the attachment to one's own body which breeds egoism. Thirdly the net effects (TS), (TI) and (EI) both influence the variable (S) not included in them. The impact of these net effects also influences the input-mix of the variable (I). The variable (S) being a self-existent entity provides neutral inputs on an interminable basis. The input-mix of the variable (I) embodying neutral inputs remains untainted by the incidence of non-neutral inputs. The input-mix registers a very high ratio of the neutral to non-neutral inputs.

In the third step the role of the variable (I) acquires great significance. The variable (I), like a processing plant, transforms the received input-mix into output-mix. The variable (I) remains unmindful about the qualities of the input and output-mix. We dwell for a while upon the quality of input-mix received by the variable (I). The contributors to the input-mix are the variables (S), (T), and (E). The Self (S) guarantees an unchanging and unceasing supply of wisdom insight and foresight including consciousness untainted by attachment and aversion. Now the contributions of the variables (T) and (E) inseparably depend upon the relation of the interaction generated between the pseudo-alive entities (entities inside the domain) and the non-alive entities (existing outside the domain). In the ego-embodied model the adaptation of ego to the propensity to passion generated compelling forces of attraction (attachment) and repulsion (aversion) through the interaction between the same noted entities. Now the ego stands acclimatized to the thought currents of purity which are either equal to or greater than (Chapter III-3) the strength of the thought currents of passion. Consequently, the variable (T) through the changed P-mix and the variable (E) through the changed E-mix provide neutral inputs to the input-mix of the variable (I). For this reason, the variables (T) and (E) reinforce and enhance the effectiveness of the neutral inputs supplied by the Self. Now the variable (I) produces output-mix identically of the same quality as the quality of the input-mix. The ratio of neutral to non-neutral inputs in the input-mix, hence the ratio of the neutral to non-neutral thought contents of activity tends to be very high. This result reverses the functional aspects of the variable (I) as noted in the ego-embodied model.

In the fourth step the impact of the key net effect (TE/ET = 1) on the net effect (IS) has to be examined. It is notable that the net effect (IS) is a summary expression of the micro order. The variable (I) represents the instruments contained in the domain of activity and the variable (S) denotes the Self as the two components of the micro order. The net effect (TE/ET = 1) directly affects the Self through (i) a decrease in the impulse of attachment, (ii) increased effectiveness of the thought currents of purity and (iii) delivery of the urge to activity from the constraining impact of attachment and egoism. The sum total of these influences also enhances the effectiveness of the Self on the working of the domain of activity.

The key net effects (TE/ET = 1) also influences the variable (S) through its impact on the variable (I). The thought currents of purity and natural ego saturate the input-mix of the variable (I) by neutral inputs. These contributions of the variables (T) and (E) accord with the neutral inputs provided by the Self. In other words, the indirect effect of the net effect (TE) infuse the input-mix with neutral inputs, which when transformed into output-mix by the variable (I) produce a high ratio of neutral to non-neutral thought contents of activity. These are attachment-disembodied thought contents of activity. That is to say, that the objects of desire and work, tangible and intangible possessions including the human body are stripped of the impulse of attachment. The supplementary impact of the net effect (TE/ET = 1) becomes operative the through the effect of the neutral thought contents of activity on each variable constituting the micro order, including the variable (I) itself.

In the first place, the likeness of the quality of neutral thought contents and the thought currents of purity reinforce the impact of the variable (T) on the micro order. Secondly, the harmony between neutral thoughts and natural ego strengthen and enhance each other to minimize the incidence of acquired ego, hence increase the effectiveness of natural ego in the micro order. Thirdly, the resulting neutral thought currents of activity act as a fastener of the thought currents of purity to the Self (S). As a result, the accelerated assimilation of the infusions of the Self by the intelligence precepts, optimal working of the instruments contained in the domain. The working of every instrument, unconstrained by attachment and egoism, ensures optimal use of the endowment of nature in the form of the instruments of activity. Finally, the optimal use of the instruments contained in the domain of activity develops I sameness between the psychonomic perspective of an individual and the Self. This is for reason of fading (Verse 14-1) of attachment of selfish-will. The minimal role of attachment, caused by its flow outside oneself, through the selflessness makes for complete non-involvement, at the subjective level. As a result, one comes to acquire almost the same attributes of that of the Self. The spirit of non-involvement promotes (Verse 18-45) spontaneous working of the micro order. One as develops in graduated steps complete control (Verse 18-33) over the working of the mind and senses which are the cause and consequence of being self-possessed. Consequently, the inputs infused by the Self motivate optimal use of the instruments of activity. The Self is established as the preceptor of the working of every instrument contained in the domain of activity. In other words, the instruments having developed immunity from the repercussions of change in the entities outside oneself tend to be controlled by the innate attribute of changelessness of the self. The entities existing inside and outside oneself subject to ceaseless change cease to disturb the intelligence through psychic swings reinforced by subjective constraints.

The received input-mix and output-mix produced by the variable (I) guarantees the optimal use of the total inputs received by the domain of activity. The stability of intelligence not only (i) secures optimal performance of each component of the variable (I) but also warrants (ii) the use of inputs of the Self in accordance with the precepts of the Self. This is conducive to exploit the innate qualities of the Self. It is explicitly noted that the best possible use of the bodily and non-bodily inputs only can secure the optimal use of all kinds of non-human capital provided by the macro order.

*　　*　　*

CHAPTER-V

SELFISH DESIRES AND THE DOMAIN OF ACTIVITY

The bondage to selfish desires is a firmly established observed phenomenon of psychonomic perspective. It is a by product of the working of the ego-embodied model (Chapter-IV-4) of a micro order. The adoption of ego to the propensity to passion catalyzes attachment, aversion, sense of self and selfish will into the domain of activity. The desire born of selfish will is the main product of the adaptation of ego to the thought currents of passion. The interactive impact between selfish desire and work provoked by it closes in complete control of the senses over the domain of activity. We propose to demonstrate (Chapter V & VI) that the two way relation between selfish desire and work impairs human welfare. To this end, we take a start with exposing (Chapter V-2) the issue of bondage to selfish desires. The selfish desires if unfulfilled plunges one into disappointment. On the contrary, its fulfillment plants addiction to the object of desire and its consequences sprout into new set of desires. Therefore, in the next step (Chapter-V-3) we specify the attributes of selfish desires to expose its non-neutral impact on the domain of activity. The selfish-will, as the root cause of selfish desires, establishes partial control of senses (Chapter-V-4) over the domain of activity by escalating the growth of non-neutral thought contents more than its neutral counterpart. The non-neutral thought contents of activity operating through each component of domain of activity (Chapter-V-5) impair human welfare. The undermining of welfare is made effective through the forces which hold intelligence in an unsettled state.

V-1 THE BONDAGE TO SELFISH DESIRES

The bondage to desire born of selfish will, called selfish desires, is an outgrowth of the working of the ego-embodied model (Chapter-IV) of the micro order. We concluded that the interactive impact of the propensity to passion and ego was the mainspring of the working of the micro order. In other words, the impact of net effect (TE/ET=1) on the working of the micro order discloses itself through its influence on the variables instruments of activity and the Self. At this stage, we limit our analysis to the impact of the said net effect on the instrument of activity, which is a proxy for the domain of activity. The impact on the Self (Chapter VI) will be considered subsequently. The thought currents of passion catalyses (Verse 3-40) the impulse of attachment and selfish desires (Verse 3-40) lodged in human ego into each component of the instruments of activity. The catalyzed mater percolates through the working of each component of the instruments of activity, hence sets the state of the domain of activity. We will try to establish that the complex results of the working of the ego-embodied model impairs (Chapter-V & VI) the welfare of individuals. The impulse of attachment reinforced by selfish desires instigates to gain for one self through one's own action. The craving to acquire stimulates the urge to action through the senses. Consequently, the domain of activity comes to be swept away by desire for the objects of senses. This amounts to partial control of the senses over the domain of activity. The domain is under complete control of the senses (Chapter-VI-2) when the urge to action closes in self serving work. At this stage our investigation is confined to partial control of the domain of activity by the senses.

The arguments presented above indicate that desires not driven by selfish will are excluded from the definition of selfish desires. The desires related to one's own subsistence and justifiable desires of others which can be accommodated within the constraint of budget are not selfish desires. The selfish will is the main product of an interaction between longing for unachieved ends and the propensity to passion. This propensity is the cause of (Verse 3-37) craving for the unachieved ends. It is also noted that (Verse 14-7) the thrust for unachieved ends gives rise to the propensity to passion. It implies that the said propensity and carving for unachieved ends are both the cause and consequence of each other. The two way causation is based upon the fact that the material and immaterial goods and services as the source of pleasure generates attachment, which through subjective valuation solidifies their importance and need. These tendencies stimulate selfish will to acquire and accumulate the objects of pleasure. Thus selfish will is the axis around which attachment chases selfish desires and selfish desires chase attachment. The selfish will grows so compelling that it outstrips one's own will power. The selfish will acts as a supplement to will power only so long as it does not subdue the will power. The selfish will constrains to think and act, as if by force, against one's own will. The selfish motive, intensified by attachment assails over thinking and action sustained by volition. One gets caught up in an unpleasant situation from which it is hard to escape. The selfish motive, in turn, increases the intensity or attachment (Chapter III) to obscure the brightness of wisdom in intelligence. Thus the intensity of attachment fixes the floor constraint which averts all effort to give up selfish will. On the contrary, the intensity of attachment also propels self-indulgence. This is the essence of the bondage to selfish desire. The willingness to free one self from selfish desires is more than offset by the willingness to self indulgence.

Let us consider the nature of self-indulgence. It reveals the essence of the trap imposed by selfish desires. We distinguish self-indulgence within oneself through brooding and actualization of self-indulgence. One can revel in pleasure born of the contact of the senses (Verse 18-38) through the senses of perception and or through the action organs. In other words, the thought and effort contents of activity (Verse 18-15) both specify action. The occurrence of thought signifies subjective action and effort making defines action in a concrete sense or objective action. It is contended that (Verse 3-6) action, either inside or outside the mind, leaves a remainder, of varying duration, as distinct from the outcome (or return) from action. It is noticeable that action so also its outcome, last for a finite length of time. But it is not true of the remainder of action. The self-indulgence engraved in the memory keeps the pleasure of gratification alive for longer length of time. The unconstrained self-indulgence within one self leaves a much more effective remainder than caused by actualized indulgence. One may refrain from action in a concrete sense, but continue self-indulgence within oneself. This explains another facet of bondage of selfish desires.

It has also to be considered why the bondage of selfish desires grows irrevocable. It is argued that an individual (Verse 5-14) himself is the architect of subjective constraints induced by selfish desire. It is notable that neither the completion of work nor its outcome generates selfish desires. It is the one's own attachment to the outcome of work that accounts for the rise of selfish desires. It is also alleged that (Verse 3-27) all kinds of work are accomplished by the nature. But the sense of self being a worker occasions one to believe that he is the work achiever. The fact of ultimate reality is that the Self activates each component of the domain of activity to perform their decreed functions through the injection of life energy. The work achiever instigated by selfish desire hatches craving for unachieved ends. The intelligence coated with the thrust for unachieved ends manifests itself as an earnest desire that whatever is desirable becomes a fact (Verse 18-17) and that is not desired never becomes a fact. The bondage of desire impels to adore that is favorable and abhor that is unfavorable. We contend that the fascination for non-alive entities obtaining outside oneself give rise to selfish desires. An intensification of selfish desires eclipses the onset of wisdom in intelligence. Consequently, intelligence comes to accommodate the impetuous behavior of the senses.

V-2 THE SPECIFIC QUALITIES OF SELFISH DESIRES

The attributes of selfish desires spring from three results derived elsewhere. In the first place, we concluded that (Chapter III) an increase in the intensity of attachment simultaneously decreases the brightness of wisdom in intelligence and increases the psychic density (burden) of thoughts. Secondly, the decision to use available means for (Chapter-III-4) for one's own welfare sets off the thought currents (Chapter III-5) of passion. Thirdly, the adaptation of ego to the thought currents of passion (Chapter IV-4) acts as a catalyzer to infuse attachment, selfish will and egoism in each component of the domain of activity. These tendencies give rise to the following attributes of selfish desires.

The selfish desires are postulated (Verse 3-37) to be most devouring. This is for the reason that self-indulgence stimulates the urge to indulge more. It is to be explicitly noted that the act of self-indulgence in the present, so also its urge in future, are in essence non-neutral in their impact. On the contrary, they both instigate zeal to action. The relation between actualization of achievement and the strategy to achieve further is rendered non-neutral because self-indulgence comes to be driven by attachment. The intemperate motivation to revel in the objects of senses causes the interactive relative relation between the actual and anticipated attainments indeterminate. The intensity of attachment to the achieved, so also to anticipated ends, makes for devouring attribute of selfish desires. The long lasting impression of joy as induced by attachment causes one's motive to be fixed in pleasure seeking. This is for the reason that the long lasting impression acts as a reaction coefficient, whose value increases when each anticipated attainment becomes a fact. This motive is the essence of most devouring attribute of selfish desires. The motive derives strength when the passion born attachment branches out into greed. The involvement in self-indulgence grows inexorable.

The selfish desires are also conjectured (Verse 3-37) to be most sinful. The selfish desire to obtain unachieved ends viewed on a sliding scale discloses that, after a limit, the expansion of selfish desire (Verse 4-17) culminates in wrongful thinking and action. To be precise, selfish desires excite longing for the gratification of the senses. Consequently, the attachment to the objects of desire, despite their being subject to ceaseless change, appear to be unchangeable. The deception of immutability of the bodily existence and objects of desire crystallizes into pleasure seeking through change. These motivations close in accumulation of long lasting psychic impressions of sins committed in the past, endorse fickleness of mind and promote ignorance. These flaws beset the psychonomic perspective. These shortcomings owe their origin to attachment of oneself to ever changing non-existent entities. The constraining influence, hence non-neutrality, arises mainly from the accumulated psychic impression of the sins committed in the past. The selfish desires are postulated to be the prime source of all sinful actions. Although it cannot be denied that thought contents of activity, embodying desires, stimulate action. But desires transmuted into selfish desires become the prime source of all sinful actions. It cannot be denied that thought contents of activity, embodying desires, stimulate action. But desires transmuted into selfish desires impel one to disregard one's own level of real permanent income, capability and eligibility to work.

The passion aroused though currents of neediness and urge to action when arbitrated by the impulse of greed obscures insight and foresight. A further increase in greed incites deception born of passivity in the psychonomic perspective. The pressure of excessive pride, arrogance and ostentatious desires push one into to the swamp of sin. The advance of the thought currents of passivity also gives rise to anti-wisdom thought contents of activity. These thought contents are extremely non-neutral degenerating life and livelihood both.

Selfish desires are postulated to concoct (Verse 3-38) incomprehensibility. The impulse of attachment to perishable objects of desire cause them to be likeable, beautiful, useful and indispensable. Thus attachment generates agreeability which concludes in selfish desires. As noted earlier (Chapter III-3) the impulse of attachment decreases brightness of wisdom in intelligence. The intelligence (Verse 18-16) is not the something as wisdom. The phenomena of wisdom, like the self-existent Self, is beginingless and everlasting. The Self diffuses insight and foresight in intelligence through wisdom. This thought current in in addition to (Chapter II-4) the stream of active consciousness. The use of the instrument called intelligence depends upon the thought currents of the propensities of passivity and purity. These thought currents respectively cause wisdom to be partially distinct, completely indistinct and completely distinct. The wisdom enveloped in selfish desire disregards the thought current of any propensity active in intelligence. Wisdom is purifier of intelligence. The impurities of psychonomic perspective are removed more by rational thinking and wisdom more than righteous action. The onset of wisdom in intelligence also dispels long lasting impression of sins, fickleness of mind and ignorance. The sinful thinking and action do not, cannot, deter the onset of wisdom. This is for reason of the intrinsic nature of wisdom. It is eternal. The subjective valuation of importance and neediness of perishable objects of desire can only temporarily envelop wisdom. The force of attachment, egoism and selfish will cannot erase the perennial flow of wisdom in the stream of active consciousness. The enveloped wisdom fosters (1) incomprehensibility regarding obligatory work and (ii) increases the impulses of selfish desires. The unintelligibility of duty and selfish desires reinforce each other to sustain the eclipse of wisdom in intelligence.

The insatiability is another (Verse 3-39) trait of selfish desires. The incidence of selfish desires becomes uncontrollable because of their being persistent in nature. The selfish desire surrounds the acquisition of objects which are essentially non-existent entities. These entities typify destruction, changeability and scarcity. The impulse of attachment fastens such objects of selfish desires to the stream of active consciousness. Furthermore, the impulse of greed and attachment add rigidity to inexorable attachment to gratify the senses. This severely constrains all effort to rescue oneself from the seize (Verse 15-5) of selfish desires. The gratification of the senses, or accumulation of wealth, or acquisition of objects of desire is not so non-neutralizing, as the desire born of selfish will. This is for the reason that selfish will is reinforced by the impulses of egoism and attachment. In fact, achievement of ends and outburst of selfish desires are both the cause and consequence of each other. The motive fixed in pleasure seeking sets up a cyclical relation between the tendency to delight and attachment to the objects of selfish desires. Let us consider the nature of such cyclical relation. The law of diminishing marginal utility and regular repetition of something in the same order creates distaste to terminate the cyclical relation. Moreover, the impulse of attachment offsets distaste to sustain the cyclical relation up to a limit only. But once the limit is reached, attachment spills over to gratify the senses from some other source. This is how fulfillment of selfish desire hatches new desires. The feeling of dissatisfaction follows distaste. The impulse of greed, working upon attachment, causes the achieved ends to grow unimportant and make unachieved ends to be significant. The selfish desires are rejuvenated by longing for created by selfish will. The selfish will internalizes attachment in the form of long lasting psychic impressions of delight experienced past, which itself sustains attachment (Verse 18-38) despite the knowledge that pleasure of contact is bound to end in separation. One grows regardless of the realized pangs of separation in the past because the anticipation of contact pleasure appears to be compelling. These tendencies sown by selfish-will sprout into insatiable selfish desires.

V-3 SELFISH DESIRES AND THE QUALITY OF THE THOUGHT CONTENTS OF ACTIVITY

It is premised that selfish desires settle the state of domain of activity through its impact on the quality of the thought contents of activity. The variables involved in the issue are the thought content of activity, its determinants and the state of micro order. Now Since the Self is beyond the reach of the domain of activity, the thought contents, in substance, are a product of and interaction between the variables ego, triad of propensities and the instruments contained in the domain, where as each is animated by the Self. It implies that the quality of thought contents reflect the prevailing conditions of the domain, whose spillover effect are upheld by the Self. Now the place of the thought contents in human activity has to be clearly spelt out. Any activity is a product (Verse 18-15) of conscious mental and or physical exertion. The thought content is primarily a product of subjective activity and effort is essentially a product of physical activity. It is suggested that the thought content of activity is the determinant of the effort content of activity. This is for reason, that the same effort content (Verse 4-16) say, an act of devotion could be motivated by faith, or selfish end, or intention to harm others. The selfish end is urged by the impulse of attachment born of passion. The intention to harm others is impelled by the obverse of attachment—that is, aversion. But the faith is beyond attachment and aversion. On this basis we distinguish between the attachment—disembodied or neutral thought contents of activity and attachment—embodied or non-neutral thought contents of activity. The various manifestations of the impulse of attachment in varying degrees in countless directions cook non-neutral thought contents of activity. These thought contents fasten the instruments contained in the domain to the Self through countless revelations of attachments. In contrast, the neutral thought contents steer the inputs provided by the Self to the instruments of activity unconstrained. This is the essence of neutral thought contents of activity. The selfish desires reflect the essential cause of non-neutrality—that is, attachment and the self-sense of one's individuality. The selfish desires are both the cause (Verse 3-37 & 14-7) and consequence of non-neutral thought contents of activity.

But it is postulated that (Verse 16-5) that the neutral and non-neutral thought contents of activity exist in the psychonomic perspective of every individual. For this reason, the operationally effective quality of thought content depends upon the ratio of the neutral to non-neutral thought contents of activity. As such we have to specify the determinants of the ratio of neutral to non-neutral thought contents of activity. In the first place, the Self, being beyond nature and its creations, infuses thought contents in the domain totally untainted by attachment or aversion. These are essentially neutral thought contents of activity. They animate the instruments contained in the domain to foster the spontaneous working of the micro order. The Self emits neutrality through (i) the voice of conscience—the undisputed source of righteousness and rationality and (ii) wisdom, insight and foresight. This constitutes the essence of absolute knowledge. It is assimilated by intelligence without the mediation of the senses on the condition that ego has accommodated the propensity to purity in a large measure. Secondly, the variables ego, triad of propensities and the instruments of activity may subscribe to a high or low ratio of the neutral to non-neutral thought contents of activity. It depends upon the texture of the key net effect, namely (TE/ET=1). Under certain conditions a simultaneous change in the composition of triad of propensities and ego mix (Chapter-IV-3) make for a high ratio of non-neutral to neutral thought contents of activity. The causative factor is the adaptation of the thought currents of passion by ego. Again the concurrent changes between P-mix and E-mix (Chapter IV-4) build a low ratio of the non-neutral to neutral thought contents of activity, for the reason of adaptation of the thought currents of purity by ego. Thirdly, it is a notable aspect that the texture of the net effect (TE/ET = 1) remains the same. In other words, the variables triad of propensities and ego retain their key character despite the correlative changes in their composition. This is the reason that the instruments contained in the domain produce a high ratio of non-neutral to neutral thought contents of activity when ego is acclimatized to the propensity to passion. As against this, the same instruments of activity generate a low ratio of non-neutral to neutral thought contents of activity if the ego is acclimatized to the propensity to purity. In either case the texture of the key net effect (TE/ET = 1) is itself an outcome of the real content of the decision made by an (Chapter III-3) by an individual. These arguments yield a significant conclusion. The unchanged and ceaseless injection of neutral thought content of activity by the Self is swayed by the attachment-embodied thought contents to cause diverse ratios of neutral to non-neutral thought contents of activity.

Having indicated the determinants of the of the ratio of neutral to non-neutral thought contents of activity, now we concentrate upon the constitution of selfish desires and its relation within the non-neutral through contents of activity. It is postulated that neutral thought contents build natural relations of psychonomic concerns. This kind of concern is generated by the Self (Verse 15-7 & 15-9) to make use of the objects of the senses though the senses and the mind. The purpose of setting up natural relations is the preservation and perpetuation of human race. The pure natural relation of concern (Verse 18-45) escalates the unconstrained working of the micro order as precepted by the Self. This kind of relation is labeled as "Unconstrained-concern". But impurity creeps into the natural relations because the decisions of an individual cease to follow the precepts of the Self. The rationality is set aside by the motives fixed in selfishness, inflated sense of oneself, short-run pleasures, self-indulgence and more than reasonable accumulation of wealth. The earnest desire for the gratification of the senses instigated by instincts and selfish-will import non-neutrality into the natural relations of concern. The unconstrained-concern gives way to "constrained-concerns".

In final analysis the non-neutrality of thought content penetrates into each component of the instruments of activity for reason of individual's decision. The decision is not averse to rectification (Chapter-VII) or its complete reversal. The radical change in perspective requires prior diagnosis of the impact of the misplaced decision. The human ego provoked by instincts, spontaneously adjusts itself to the thought currents of the propensity to passion. The propensity (Verse 14-7) being attachment incarnate, excites (Interpretation of reality and sense of self) selfish will. It is emphasized that the interactive impact between attachment and egoism, made functional by selfish will, instigates indeterminate desire for self-indulgence. But we contend that attachment, egoism and selfish will do not, by themselves, bring their non-neutral impact on the thought content of activity. We conjecture a critical minimum level (or intensity) of selfish will necessary to sustain unconstrained natural relations of concern. The decisions fixed in the motive of pleasure seeking causes the actual level of selfish will to overshoot its critical minimum level that neutrality gives way to non-neutrality. The impulse of attachment and selfish desires, being the cause (Verse 14-7) and consequence (Verse 3-37) of each other tend to intensify selfish will fueled by the manifestations attachment and sense of self in varying degrees in multiple directions. Selfish will like an autocrat, urges all its manifestations to make non-neutrality known to the domain of activity. The manifestations of selfish will are selfish desires, anger, arrogance, excessive pride and self-styled notion of elite. The uncontrollable selfish desires disembark one into the web of indeterminate (Verse 16-12) expectations and limitless (verse 16-11) care, anxiety and distress. These attributes of non-neutrality emerge from and end in the urge to enjoy pleasures made known by the senses. The entire psychonomic perspective smeared by (Verse 16-16) delusion born on ignorance impels one to be bounded by the bodily and worldly concerns. The greed motivated comprehension (Verse 16-7) fails to distinguish between the areas where to abstain from concern and action and where to accept the same. The personal nature grows impure—that is, burdened with attachment and aversion, which constitutes the axis of selfish desires and non-neutral thought contents of activity. Each form of selfish will unfolds its non-neutral impact on the thought contents of activity in specific way. Selfish will interferes with the natural functioning (Verse 18-45) of micro order in three different ways. In the first place, the entry of attachment, aversion and selfish desires (Verse 3-34 & 3-40) taints the working of each component of the instrument of activity. The negative thinking is provoked by aversion preventing the good aspects to be exposed and attachment preventing the bad aspects to be disclosed. Thus aversion and attachment are respectively biased in favour of bad and good attributes of persons, goods and things. The phenomena of duality or the coexistence of (Verse 2-45) equally relevant opposite stands deepens the constrained-concern. Secondly, each component of the instrument of activity preoccupied with selfish desires, greed, anger etc amounts to unwarranted use of the inputs provided by the Self. This tendency closes in careless use of the energy, consciousness and knowledge diffused by the self. Thirdly, the use of inputs provided by the Self end in suboptimal performance of each component of the instrument of activity. In view of these arguments we infer that the intensity of selfish will makes the ratio of non-neutral to neutral thought contents of activity determinate. An increase (decrease) in the intensity of selfish will decreases (increases) the content of neutrality in the thought contents of activity.

V-4 THE STATE OF DOMAIN OF ACTIVITY

The domain of activity comprises ego, intelligence, mind and the senses. The ego, on the instance of human decision, adapts itself either to the thought currents (Chapter IV-4 & IV-5) of passion or purity. Therefore, the triad of propensities cannot be included as a component of the domain of activity.

Similarly, the senses carry out the directives issued by the ego, intelligence and mind, hence cannot be adopted as the leading component. Therefore, the key component can either be the intelligence or the mind. In other words, the state of the domain of activity depends either on the stability of intelligence or that of mind. The text rejects mind as the key component for the following reasons. A stable mind would suspend all activities performed by the organs of action. Moreover, the innate fickleness of the mind (Verse 6-36) would frequently upset its attained stability. It is well known that an effort to turn away from the thought currents occupying the mind causes fixation in the same thought currents. The stability of mind is essentially temporary but useful in day to day dealing in life. But one stable in intelligence is resolute in thought and steadfast in decisions. The primary functions of the intelligence are rational decision making. It is encouraged by the long lasting stability of intelligence. The stability of intelligence lasts much longer (Verse 2-55) as compared to that of mind. Thus we suggest that the state of domain activity is mainly influenced by intelligence.

It is subsequently demonstrated (Chapter VII) that the steady state of intelligence is the passageway to welfare presently we will consider the state of intelligence, hence of the domain of activity, in the context where ego accommodates the thought currents of passion. The rank of (Chapter-II-5) ego is higher than intelligence, but lower as compared to the Self. It means that ego, as an internal instrument of activity, determines (i) the use of inputs provided by the Self and (ii) issues directives to the intelligence regarding the direction of employment of input provided by nature and input received from the Self. Let us consider how ego regulates the use of total inputs. The use of neutral inputs received by ego from the Self is tampered by attachment, aversion and sense of self to pacify the senses. Consequently, natural ego dominated by passion grows defenseless against the constrained relations of concern produced by attachment, aversion and egoism. Thus each component of the instrument of activity is impelled, as if by force, to use the total inputs to foster gratification of the senses and accumulation of wealth. The urge to self-indulgence and urge to self-seeking work travel through the mind and the senses because wisdom (Chapter III-3) stands eclipsed by attachment and immoderate sense of self. Thus the direct impact of ego and the indirect impact of self-indulgence is to unsettle the intelligence.

It would be instructive to consider the repercussions of the intensified urge to self-indulgence on intelligence, hence on the domain of activity. The said urge generates two tendencies which render intelligence unsettled. In the first place, the motive fixed in pleasure seeking provokes the senses for instantaneous contact with the objects of sense. The inexorable fascination for the objects of sense saps the control of mind over the senses and their objects. The mind comes to be controlled by the senses. The mind ceases to monitor the senses. The sequence of (Chapter II-5) strongly ordering in the micro order is reversed. Secondly, since the selfish will is lodged in ego, even after the act of self—indulgence (Verse

3-3-40) cease to be fact, it continues to motivate indulgence over any length of time in future.

One may turn the senses and the mind away from (Verse 2-58) self-indulgence. Yet its traces in the form of selfish will would force one to act against (Verse 2-59) one's own will. It is alleged that (Verse 2-60) the impetuous senses outwit even the self-possessed to indulge in the objects of senses. This is for the reason that intelligence remains preoccupied with bodily and worldly concerns. Consequently, till the residues of contact pleasure remain alive and long lasting psychic impressions of self-indulgence persist, one continues to be subdued by the senses. The senses cease to be under self—control. One tends to be controlled by the senses. It is pointed out that as the impetuous senses abduct the mind, and the mind (Verse 6-36) spirits away the intelligence. The attachment to the object of a given single sense (Verse 2-67) is equally powerful to force the mind to come after it.

The partial control of the senses closes in unsettled intelligence which in final analysis fixes the state of the domain of activity. The domain is also influenced by selfish desires which urge the intensity of attachment to transmute (Chapter III-3) the propensity to passion into passivity. The merger of passion into passivity engenders a qualitative change in the non-neutral thought content of activity. The continued thinking, anchored in attachment, about earthly gains hatches brooding which cycles and recycles the motive fixed in pleasure seeking. The phenomena of selfish desires come to be precepted by greed—that is, the urge to acquire more than is right and reasonable. Consequently, the delay and or the threat of non-fulfillment of selfish desires evoke anger. The episode of anger is a mixed (Verse 2-62) manifestation of the propensities of passion and passivity. In fact, desires, anger, greed, and sense of ownership breed delusion born of passivity. The delusion, depending upon its cause, generates different kinds of reactions. The delusion caused by selfish desires impels one to carry out uncalled for work for the reason of eclipsed wisdom. The delusion caused by anger instigates an impertinent behavior towards seniors and elders. The delusion caused by greed blurs the distinction between truth and falsehood, between right and wrong-hence motivates gains through wrong means. In the same way, attachment to the sense to ownership provokes partiality and discrimination as blinded by delusion. Thus the motive fixed in pleasure seeking and selfishness generates non-neutral thoughts through selfish desires, anger, greed and urge to ownership. The merger of the propensity to passion into passivity closes in delusion which destroys insight and foresight rendering unsettled intelligence.

The arguments of the preceding sections give rise to twin unavoidable consequences. In the first place all objects of self-indulgence are lifeless entities and subject to continual change. They are the means of short-lived cycles of joy and sorrow. In comparisons to this the Self is a self-existent entity. The Self despite being an embodiment of changelessness is an alive entity. It is self evident that the Self can be pacified only through Self. The thrust for enduring contentment, peace and happiness of one engrossed in change remains unquenched over whole life span.

Secondly, it is alleged that (Verse 14-7 and 5-22) that the end result of self-indulgence, as impelled by passion, is sorrow. The gratification of the senses (Verse 18-38) is highly pleasing to begin with but unpleasant to end with. This is for the reason that self-indulgence involves loss of life energy and separation from the object of self-indulgence. The demonstration effect emitted by different standards of living cause misery and heart-break to those placed at lower standard of living. They are oppressed by an imagined notion of misfortune. Similarly, the non-availability of the desired object of indulgence or longing for indulgence associated with incompetence to indulge and threat of separation plunges one into grief and tribulation. The impact of desires on the domain of activity is impelled to function as precepted by the senses. In the following chapter we will consider the repercussion of work stimulated by selfish desires on the domain of activity. The selfish desires and self-seeking work interacting upon each other end in complete control of the senses over the domain of activity.

*   *   *

CHAPTER-VI

THE CONSTRAINED CONCERN AND HUMAN ACTIVITY

The relations of concern forced by the desire and work born of selfish-will close in constrained human activity. The desire and work both subdued by selfish-will makes the attachment-embodied thoughts and impulse of attachment as the cause and consequence of each other. This sets the stage (Chapter VI—1) for non-neutral psychonomic perspective. The notable aspect of the perspective is that the consequence of non-neutrality is itself changes into the cause of non-neutrality. An incisive examination of the reciprocal relation between selfish-will and impure nature of individuals (Chapter VI-2) reveals the existence of the phenomena of internalization of attachment. The work adapted to gratify selfish-will delimits the size of work portfolio. As a result, the amount of efflux of attachment though work for the welfare of others lags far behind the amount of influx of attachment inside the domain of activity. This explains the essence of the phenomena of internalization of attachment. The internalized attachment generates subjective constraints (Chapter VI—3), psychic oscillations (Chapter VI-4) and underutilization (Chapter VI-5) of human capital. The subjective cause and subjective consequence created by exclusive concern for oneself explains the phenomena of subjective constraints. The subjective constraints use the string of egoism and attachment to channel life energy, knowledge and consciousness to foster selfish-will. Again, the exclusive concern, in any measure, for oneself connects the world outside to the world inside oneself. For this reason, the unceasing change occurring outside oneself infuses (Chapter VI-4) unstable psychonomic perspective inside oneself. As a result individuals experience cycles of pleasure and pain, fulfillments and frustrations etc. Finally, we find that the use of the available means—that is, inputs provided by the Self (called primary human capital) and that the instruments endowed by nature contained in the domain of activity (called secondary human capital) results in underutilization of human capital. The use of available means for oneself ceases in suboptimal use of the instruments contained in the domain and a failure to exploit the innate qualities of the Self. This is for reason that internalization of attachment imposes subjective constraints and psychic oscillation on the psychonomic perspective.

VI-1 THE NON-NEUTRAL PERSPECTIVE

The background of the non-neutral psychonomic perspective was stipulated (Chapter IV-4) by the ego-embodied model of the micro order. The adaptation of human ego to the propensity to passion was listed as the mainspring influencing the input-mix received and output-mix produced by the instruments of activity. Accordingly, the impact of the interaction between ego and thought currents of passion on the instruments of activity brought forth attachment-embodied thought contents of activity. It is called, non-neutral thought contents of activity. As a result, the correlative relation between selfish-will and selfish desire closing in non-neutral thought contents (Chapter V-2) of activity, establish the non-neutral psychonomic perspective. The same line of reasoning can be pressed forward to point out additional causes and consequences of the non-neutral psychonomic perspective. The selfish-will not only provokes selfish desires, but also stimulates self-serving work to fulfill selfish desires. It is further argued that selfish desires and selfish work reinforce each other to solidify the (Chapter VI-2) the impure nature of individuals. The selfish-will and impure personal nature steps up the interaction between selfish desires and selfish work. This occasions the impulse of attachment to rotate inside the domain of activity. It is also shown (Chapter VI-2) that the rotation of attachment gives rise to tendencies which cause the flow of attachment into the domain to prevail over the attachment flowing outside the domain. The resulting internalized attachment itself emerges as an independent factor to establish non-neutral psychonomic perspective. A notable aspect of the perspective is that the non-neutral thought contents of activity prevail over the neutral thought contents of activity. This constitutes the essence of the non-neutral psychonomic perspective.

A few comments are in order to place the subsequent arguments in the right perspective. We recall a few facts of ultimate reality (Chapter II-5) noted earlier. In the first place, the primary human capital (inputs provided by the Self) animates the instruments (secondary human capital) of activity. Secondly, the self remains entirely untainted (Verse 13-31 & 13-32) by the activities accomplished by the instruments contained in the domain of activity. Thirdly, the domain of activity is the final user of the inputs received from the Self and nature. The instruments contained in the domain are the endowment of nature. For this reason, full or underutilization of human capital (Chapter VI-5) depends upon the 'mode of use' of the inputs created by and used for the working of the micro order.

However, the operation of the micro order is significantly influenced by the net effect produced by ego (Chapter IV-3) adapted to the propensity to passion. In this regard it is necessary to lay down the role of the impulse of attachment in the working of the micro order. We recall that an immoderate increase in the level (or intensity) of attachment (Chapter III-2) transforms the propensity to passion into passivity and its non-appearance converts the propensity to passion into purity. The same impulse in its moderate role acts as an adhesive. It ties down the object of attachment to the instruments of activity through the stream of active consciousness. For this reason, the level of attachment needed to perform its adhesive role may be accepted as its natural level. But the motives of individuals fixed in pleasure seeking, selfishness and self-indulgence induces the level (intensity) of attachment to overshoot its natural level. The extent of deviation of the impulse of attachment from its natural level is an indicator of the incidence of non-neutrality in the psychonomic perspective. The phenomena of overshooting of attachment are hypothesized to close in constrained human activity (Chapter VI-3 & VI-4) and underutilization of (Chapter VI-5) human capital. The next chapter (Chapter VII) would seek a solution as to how the overshooting of attachment can be eliminated to restore (Verse 18-45) the natural working of micro order.

VI-2 THE INTERNALIZATION OF ATTACHMENT

The term internalization of attachment refers to the amount of inward flow of attachment into the domain in excess of its outward flow from the domain. The enquiry into the causes and consequences of the phenomena must begin with who internalizes attachment inside the domain? The analytical framework (Chapter II-5) of the micro order comprises the "alive entity" and "pseudo-alive entities". The Self an alive entity, is beyond the ceaseless change that occurs outside as well as inside the domain. Similarly, the non-alive entities, existing outside the domain, are devoid of consciousness, hence incapable of fixing relations either with the alive or pseudo-alive entities. This means that neither the Self nor non-alive entities are instrumental in inducing the internalization of attachment. These facts ascertain that pseudo-alive and non-alive entities acting upon each other account for internalization of attachment inside the domain. Briefly speaking, the phenomena of internalization can be established by looking at first the state of pseudo-alive entities. In the next step the action and counteraction between the pseudo-alive and non-alive entities can be scrutinized to specify the cause of internalization.

Therefore we begin with the evaluation of the state of pseudo-alive entities existing inside the domain. These entities are the instruments, not as the cause, of internalization of attachment. But we know (Chapter III-3 & IV-3) that the adaptation of the thought currents of passion by ego triggers significant changes in the working of instruments ranked lower than ego in the domain. The thought currents of passion activate the impulse of attachment (Verse 3-434) and desire born of selfish-will (Verse 3-40) sheltered in itself. As a result the self-sense of one's individuality and attachment to work interact to induce rotation of attachment between the two axes situate inside the domain of activity. The two axes are the selfish-will and impure personal nature of individuals. The attachment embodied (non-neutral) thought content of activity connects the two axes. The selfish will solidifies into personal nature through attachment embodied thought content of activities. And the impure personal nature strengthens selfish will again through the same kind of thought content of activity. Accordingly, the relation between the attachment embodied thought content of activity and the impulse of attachment determine the modus operandi of rotation of attachment inside the domain of activity.

Let us examine how the motive of selfish-will generates impure personal nature through the attachment-embodied (or non-neutral) thought contents of activity. The selfish-will operating through (i) the motive of self-indulgence urges selfish desires, (desires born of selfish-will). The selfish-will again acting through (ii) an immoderate self-sense of being a worker urges work to gratify selfish desires. It is notable that the pseudo-alive entities, existing inside the domain, remain preoccupied with three kinds of self-sustaining cause-effect relationship namely between (a) selfish desires and self-indulgence, (b) self-serving work and egoism and (c) selfish desires and self-serving work. The relationship (a) becomes effective through attachment to self-indulgence which excites selfish desires and selfish desires foster self-indulgence to secure selfish-will. The relationship (b) becomes effective through attachment to the self-sense of being a worker inducing self-serving work and work in turn fosters selfish-will through the self-sense of being and activity-achiever. These two self-sustaining cause-effect relations enhance and re-enforce each other to make various manifestations of attachment, in varying degrees in countless directions. The attachment is thus well—founded in the psychonomic perspective. In other words, selfish desires stimulate self-serving work and latter yields the fruit of selfish desires. It is observed that in any case the attachment—embodied thought contents of activity to gratify personal desires, stimulates its counterpart—the effort content of activity. We conclude that the attachment-embodied, or non-neutral, thought contents of activity provide the leverage to the rotation of attachment through selfish-will operating both through the thought and effort contents of activity. The selfish-will occupies the one end of the axis of rotation of attachment inside the domain of activity.

The other end of the axis of rotation of attachment is the impure personal nature of individuals. The impure personal nature is to be accepted as the creation of selfish-will. The adaptation of the thought currents of passion by ego causes attraction (attachment) and its obverse (Verse 3-34) repulsion (aversion) to be embedded in ego. As a result egoism in turn permanently secures attachment and aversion in ego. This phenomenon renders personal nature impure through three distinct routes. In the first place, the impulses of attachment provoke attraction to merge into psychic-fixation. As a result, the force of attachment expels any concern other than the object of attachment from the mind. In addition to it, the mind experiences the thought about the object of attachment strongly with unwanted persistency. Secondly, the psychonomic perspective comes to be tainted by attachment-caused agreeability and aversion-caused disagreeability. The agreeability focuses on the positive or appealing attributes of the object of attachment and conceals its negative attributes. And the aversion-caused disagreeability focuses on the negative or unappealing attributes of the object of aversion and hides its positive attributes. The incidence of such distortions in perception is an indicator of deviations from rational behavior. The branching out of attachment, so also of aversion, caused by non-neutral thought contents of activity, specify the texture of impure personal nature of individuals. Thirdly, the ego as an instrument of activity is the prime mover of the domain of activity. It infuses (Verse 3-34) attachment and aversion into every other instrument ranked lower than itself in the domain of activity. Consequently, the appearance of attachment (aversion) in intelligence causes concern for one's own stand but unconcern for other's point of view. The sight of attachment (aversion) causes one to adore that appeal to mind, but abhor that is unappealing to mind. The entry of attachment (aversion) in the senses causes inclination towards objects friendly to the senses but disinclination towards the objects unfriendly to the senses. The impulses of attachment (aversion) also induce attraction and repulsion among the objects of the senses—that is, sight, sound, smell, tastes and touch. Briefly speaking, the impulses of attachment (aversion) precept the operations of the two internal instruments of activity, five senses and the five objects of the senses. As such constrained-concern born of attachment, so also aversion, induce (i) involuntary tendencies to act constantly in a certain manner. In other words, the nature of individuals tainted by attachment and aversion grows impure. Yet another reason for the emergence of impure personal nature is (ii) that the force of selfish-will subdues the will power. Consequently, selfish-will overshadows the brightness of insight and foresight in intelligence. The cause-effect relationship between action and thoughts induced by attachment-embodied (or non-neutral) thought contents of activity crystallize into impure nature of individuals.

The issue of rotation of attachment inside the domain requires us to demonstrate the impact of impure personal nature on selfish-will. The never ending cyclical relation between selfish desires and self-seeking work merges impure personal nature into selfish-will. The two become indistinguishable. The frequent repetition of involuntary tendencies under the constant pressure of selfish motive and egoism, generate 'constrained-concern' both in thought and action. The entire working of the micro order comes to be controlled by constrained-concern born of (Chapter V-3) non-neutral thought contents of activity. These thought contents overshadow the brightness of insight and foresight in intelligence. Consequently, the actions impelled by the impulse of attachment and thought contents of activity, as the cause and consequence of each other, solidify into self-sustaining (Chapter VI-3) long-lasting psychic impressions. In other words the merger of personal nature into selfish-will closes in a large (Chapter VI-3) sized bundle of unyielding subjective constraints.

Now we can dwell upon how the merger of impure personal nature into selfish-will set up a mechanism to induce a large amount of flow of attachment inside the domain in excess of the amount of flow of attachment outside the domain. The co-operators in the mechanism are the pseudo-alive and non-alive entities. Briefly speaking, the pseudo-alive entities project the impulse of attachment toward the non-alive entities and the non-alive entities rebound attachment towards the pseudo-alive entities. The crucial aspect of the functioning of internalization of attachment starts from the senses at the tail end of the pseudo-alive entities. The senses, drawing impetus from the merger of personal nature into selfish-will, project the impulse of attachment outside the domain. This is crowding-out of attachment. The crowded-out attachment acts as sensors of the non-alive entities. The information collected by the sensors is subjectively evaluated by the internal instruments of activity, namely ego, intelligence an mind. The selfish will merged into impure personal nature precepts the evaluation of information about the non-alive entities. The precepted subjective evaluation builds the weekly ordered preference map of an individual as a result the preference map grows as an independent variable to crowed the impulse of attachment outside the domain, as well as crowed in the attachment inside the domain. The notable aspect of the sequence of internalization is that the amount of crowed out attachment is significantly small in amount as compared to the amount of crowed out of attachment. This is for the reason that the use of available means assigns large weightage to selfish desires as gratification senses rather than the use of means for the betterment of others. The conclusion of the forgoing arguments is that the rotation of attachment inside the domain accounts for recurring internalization of attachment.

VI-3 THE CONCEPT OF SUBJECTIVE CONSTRAINTS

The preceding section has established that the dual rotation of attachment, inside oneself, ingrains domain of activity with attachment to entities obtaining outside one-self. The consequent large and continuous inflow of attachment crystalizes into, what we label as subjective constraints. The cause and the consequences of the constraints are subjective in substance. The subjective constraints are premised (Chapter-V-2) to originate from attachment to non-alive entities which is reflected in and result in non-neutral thought contents of activity. Now we proceed to consider the formation of subjective constraints and its impact on the domain of activity.

Let us consider the genesis of formation of subjective constraints. The first aspect of the mechanism is the harmonious changes (Chapter-IV-4) between the composition of ego and the composition of the thought currents of the triad of propensities. In the present context the decision to use available means (Chapter-III-4) for one's own welfare acclimatizes ego to thought currents of passion more than the thought currents of the other two propensities. The thought currents of passion in turn diffuse the intrinsic characteristics of ego to each component of the instrument of activity. The acquired ego is postulated to shelter attachment (Verse-3-34) and selfish (Verse-3-40) desire. Thus the propensity to passion, being attachment incarnate, assumes its concrete from through ego. It implies that ego accommodates the impulses of attachment and aversion and these impulses strengthen the hold of ego on each component of the instruments of activity. Consequently, the influence of these impulses on intelligence cause one's own ideas, convictions and assertions to be appealing, but the same coming from others becomes unappealing. The appearance of the same impulses in mind cause agreeable situations, events and circumstances to be pleasant but disagreeable conditions unpleasant. Finally, the entry of these impulses in the senses create taste for everything suited to the senses, but distaste for those unsuited to the senses. The impulses of attachment and aversion manifest themselves thought the objects of the senses, namely, sight, sound, smell, taste and touch. Accordingly, the objects of the senses create pleasant or unpleasant reaction. Therefore, we conclude that the debut of attachment and aversion in the intelligence, mind and objects of the senses generate concerns as constrained by them. The subjective constraints thus constituted, interfere with the natural functioning of the intelligence, mind and the senses.

Thus the subjective constraints can be defined as an irresistible urge, operative inside oneself, within an enclosed framework, so as to precept the use of received subjective inputs, by an individual, in a particular direction only. The suggested definition of subjective constraint warrants an explanation as to (i) why the urge to subjective activity becomes irresistible, (ii) the meaning of enclosed framework and (iii) how the subjective constraints percept the use of received subjective inputs in a particular direction only. The third issue will be taken up (Chapter-VI-5) subsequently. The first issues can be explained by using the analogy of a knot. The string used to tie a knot accounts for the irresistible urge to mental action. And the looping of the string describes the enclosed framework within which the subject constraints get crystalized.

The string is composed of three strong interweaved threads namely, the impulse of attachment, the sense of self (egoism) and selfish will. It selfish will arise first, attachment and self-sense follow the track. Similarly, if attachment takes a lead the other two threads drift along to seize the object of attachment. Finally, the rise of self-sense instantly subdues attachment and selfish will to follow its pathway. It is observed that each thread of the string incites an irrevocable drive to subjective activity only in a specific direction. The string impels strict adherence to the object of attachment and resist its separation. An increase in the incidence of the above noted tendencies of selfish will, beyond a limit, suppresses the will power. The selfish will generates compelling forces to indulge in subjective activity, in a given direction, even against one's own will. An increase in the sense of self makes one head-strong to remain occupied in a particular direction only. The joint impact of the three threads reduces flexibility in subjective activity. The subjective activity in a particular direction solidifies as constrained-concern.

Now we can consider the second aspect of the concept of subjective constraints. It is looping of the string. The act of looping specifies the nature of enclosed framework. We have seen earlier (Chapter VI-3) how the rotation of attachment inside the domain internalizes attachment through a particular mechanism. The mechanism was shown to be built by the reciprocal action between selfish-will and subjective valuation of entities existing outside the domain. The extended form of the same mechanism explains the episode of looping. In the first place, the mechanism operating through the senses, projects attachment outside the domain into the world of non-alive entities. Now the sense of agreeability and disagreeability, ingrained in human nature when projected outside oneself provides data for constituting the weakly ordered preference map inside the domain. Secondly, the ordered preference map, embodying selfish-will and subjective valuation of non-alive entities cause these entities to recoil the impulse of attachment through the senses. The episode of looping revolves around the senses.

The creation of a 'lump' is the final aspect of the formation of subjective constraints. The subjective constraints, like a lump, are to be viewed as a 'residue' of the constrained-concern caused by the attachment-embodied subjective activity. Any activity after its completion and return after its consumption leaves behind a residue called 'lasting psychic impression'. This is for the reason that ego as the abode of attachment and egoism (Verse 3-40) generates attachment-embodied thought contents of activity—the cause of subjective activity. While the activity and its consequences are short-lived, the residue lodged in ego continues to stimulate the currents of activity of similar kind in future. The suggested theoretical construct (Chapter IV-4 & IV-5) also supports the rise of residue or subjective constraints. We have seen how the output-mix produced by the instruments of activity also influences the working of each instrument of activity, contained in the domain. The impulses that generate the attachment-embodied thought contents of activity regenerate themselves to become self-sustaining. This phenomenon intensifies the upsetting impact in the micro order. We contend that overshooting of the actual level of attachment over its natural level insights its binding power. The psychonomic perspective comes to be sandwiched between the ceiling or upper bound constraint and the floor or lower bound constraint. The upper and lower bound constraints respectively index the extent of thrust of attachment and extent of resistance to abandon attachment. An increase in the level (or Intensity) of attachment not only raises the height of the upper bound constraint, but pulls the lower bound constraint near and nearer to itself. The merger of upper and lower bound constraints closes in psychic-fixation. The adaptive faculty of individuals tightly holds (Verse 18-34) the attachment-embodied thought contents of activity, which monitors the functioning of intelligence. These tendencies force to cling to money and wealth to perform even righteous purposes for selfish ends and self-indulgence.

We can say something more about the nature of the residue or subjective constraints. In the first place, the reciprocal relation between the attachment-embodied thought and effort contents of activity generate 'attachment-constraints'. For the same reason the correlative relation (Verse 18-14) between the aversion-embodied thought and effort contents of activity give rise to 'aversion-constraints'. The motive underlying the attachment and aversion constraints could be either for a right or wrong cause. Secondly, even though aversion-constraint for selfish reasons may impel one to abstain (Verse 18-38) from action, the attachment-constraint may be strong enough to excite action. In the same way, constraint born of aversion may prevail over the attachment-constraint; hence for some selfish reason inhibit action. Thirdly, subjective constraints indexing long lasting psychic impressions may, or may not, entail the binding impact of attachment. In other words, the lasting psychic-impressions may, or may not, cause bondage to action—or constrained activity. The reason being that the adaptation of ego to the propensity to purity causes its thought currents to become effective, hence modify the incidence of passion on ego. As a result, the net impact of passion and purity is to create the lasting psychic-impressions of purity, without the appearance of the binding impact of attachment. The underlying fact is that while the urge to action, born of the propensity to passion, continues to be effective, the overshooting impact of attachment (Chapter VII) ceases to be operative. For this reason, the lasting psychic-impression and the binding impact of attachment increasingly increases as the propensity to passion (Chapter III-2) merges into passivity. Finally, the lasting psychic-impression, so also the bind of attachment, stimulates action (Verse 18-14) in embryonic form in future. The strength of reaction in future depends upon the intensity, depth and duration of the impact of attachment on ego, intelligence and mind.

VI-4 THE PHENOMENA OF PSYCHIC OSCILLATIONS

The preceding section (Chapter VI-3) explained how the internalization of attachment concludes in subjective constraints. The internalization of attachment also gives rise to the phenomena of psychic-oscillations through the correlative repercussions between the attachment-embodied thought contents of activity and the impulse of attachment. Individuals helplessly experience happiness and unhappiness, delight and anguish, blessedness and hardship etc. At the first sight one may endorse the cause of joy and sorrow to be exogenously determined. This is for reason of availability or non-availability of work material, opportunity to work, completion or non-completion of work and uncertainty about the size, composition and time-shape of returns. The success or failure, gain or loss, or occupation or defeat are certainly exogenously determined and are non-manipulable. This is a fact of life reality. But it is also a fact that all that occurs outside the domain does not generate oscillations in the psychic state. This is for the reason that outside the domain is the world of entities devoid of consciousness. These are non-alive entities— incapable of bringing up relation of concern with entities inside the domain. This argument establishes that the cause of psychic oscillations must be sought inside—rather than outside, the domain. Individuals contrive linkage between entities existing outside and inside the domain. The linkage between the two kinds of entities is not natural. It is man made.

This stage of enquiry needs us to specify the agency responsible for the said linkage—made inside the domain. The Self is the seat of consciousness. It establishes the relations of concern with all kinds of entities (Verse 15-7) through the instruments of activity contained in the domain. But the Self as the epitome of changelessness perceives psychic oscillations, hence does not cause oscillations. The entity next to the Self is human ego. The ego as the authority of contrived relations (Chapter II-3) not only mediates between the Self (Chapter II-5) and the domain but also between the entities existing outside and inside the domain through the pseudo-alive entities. It appears to be the cause of psychic oscillations. But ego is merely an instrument of activity. The ego accommodates the thought currents of passion or purity (Chapter III-3) subject to the decision of an individual. The decision to use the available means for selfish ends impels ego to accommodate the thought currents of passion. This move of ego brings forth (Chapter VI-3) internalization of attachment as the exclusive source of disturbances in the micro order.

The preceding arguments identify human decision to be the causative factor of psychic oscillations. Individuals themselves author psychic oscillations. The byproduct of this authorship is the adaptation of ego to passion which makes the binding power of attachment effective. It is premised that joy and sorrow—both are a consequence of attachment and its obverse aversion. The association with the object of attachment, so also disengagement with the object of aversion causes joy. As against this, the disassociation with the object of attachment, so also engagement with the object of aversion gives rise to sorrow. These contentions fix the psychonomic bases of motivations to maximize that is agreeable and minimize that is disagreeable to secure the best possible out of life and livelihood. These notions build the relation of 'constrained-concern'— concerns guarded on both sides by attachment and aversion. Such concerns generate (Verse 12-17) reaction of elation when the desired is actualized and downcast when undesirable becomes a fact.

We can now specify the psychonomic causes of psychic oscillations in more concrete terms. We emphasize that the thought—not the effort content of activity, is relevant for analysis. The effort simply (Verse 14-16) actualizes the thought contents of activity—a change in the thought content alters the true complexion of effort content of activity. The thought content of activity is fabricated by the phenomena (Chapter VI-3) of internalization of attachment inside the domain of activity. As a result, the give and take between the attachment-embodied thought contents and the impulse of attachment align the natural urge (Verse 3-5) to action (i) to gratify the senses on the assumption that (ii) work actualizes unachieved ends (iii) hence self-seeking work (iv) blows up the self-sense of being a worker. Accordingly, the network of subjective constraints is caused by attachment to the size, composition and time-shape of returns. The attachment arising from attachment to return spills over into the constraint born of exaggerated sense of ownership of the instruments of activity contained in the domain. The outgrowth of constraints related to return and ownership of instruments of activity close in another cause of psychic oscillation that is the pride of being an activity-achiever.

VI-5 THE UNDERUTILIZATION OF HUMAN CAPITAL

The existence of an individual comprises his body and the soul. These components of existence constituting the micro order are respectively labeled as the secondary and primary human capital. The secondary human capital contains a variety of instruments contained in the domain of activity as endowed by nature. The primary human capital is the Self.

It is postulated to be (Verse 15-7) a fraction of the Supreme Self. The thought and effort contents of activity evidence the produce of human capital. These products energize the dynamic changes in the world outside and inside oneself. The working of micro order depends upon the mode of use (Chapter III-3) of the inputs provided by the Self and nature. The optimal use of these inputs brings about full utilization of human capital. Accordingly, the suboptimal use of these inputs occasions underutilization of human capital. It is put forward as a hypothesis that the suboptimal use of the instruments contained in the domain give rise to lack of exploitation of the potentialities of the Self.

To test the validity of the hypothesis we transcribe a postulate (Verse 6-6) in terms of the results derived earlier from the ego-embodied (Chapter IV-3) and egoless (Chapter IV-4) models of micro order. It is premised that if the relative impact of synchronous change in the composition of the triad of propensities and ego, on the instruments contained in the domain, exceeds that on the Self then the dynamic pressures originating in the domain would prevail over the Self. Consequently, the domain would subdue the Self causing (Chapter VI-5) suboptimal use of human capital. Secondly, in the opposite context (Chapter VII-6) the overriding influence of the Self on the domain would bring about full utilization of human capital.

Our present concern is how the pressures originating in the domain overcome the Self to bring about underutilization of human capital. For this reason, we begin with the criterion of full utilization of human capital. The optimal use of inputs (any work material) evidences its full utilization. The optimal test of efficiency requires that the completion or non-completion, so also receipt or non-receipt of return from work (Verse 2-50) does not upset the psychic-equilibrium (or balanced inner self) of the worker. This is for the reason that attachment to work and or attachment to its return induces up-swing in case of successful completion of work and or desired receipt of return. The opposite conditions of non-completion of work and or non-receipt of the desired return induce a down swing. The unsteady inner self is a definite indicator of suboptimal use of inputs used in the work.

Now we can work out the premise that the pressures originating in the domain cause suboptimal use of the instruments of activity, which bring about a failure to capitalize on the potentialities of the Self. The relation set up by the Self with the domain is upheld as the cause of suboptimal use of human capital. This is untenable. The Self is a self-existent entity. It is beyond the nature born impulses of attachment and aversion. The relations set up by the Self are natural. They function as a conduit between the Self and the domain. The motives of selfishness fixed in pleasure seeking and self—indulgence pollute the natural relation set up by the Self. These motives escalate the actual level (or intensity) of attachment over its (Chapter VI-1) natural level. The extent of overshot level of attachment impairs the strength of the influence of the Self over the secondary human capital (or instruments contained in the domain). As a result, the highly restrictive impact of attachment directly arrests the entities contained inside and outside the domain. The repercussions following the interaction (Chapter II-5) between these entities seized by attachment diffuse their indirect influence on the Self as well. The inexorable restive impact of attachment is singled out as the cause of suboptimal use of the secondary human capital (the instruments contained in the domain).

The next step is to consider is how the impulse of attachment urges suboptimal use of instruments of activity. The motives born of selfish-will acclimatize ego to the propensity to passion. Consequently, ego injects countless manifestations of attachment (Verse 3-34) and selfish-will (Verse 3-40) into each instrument contained in the domain. The impulse of attachment, selfish-will and excessive pride of one's individuality concludes in suboptimal use of the instruments contained in the domain. Thus in the first place, the entry of attachment encourages each instrument to disclose the positive attributes of the object of attachment, but cover up their negative attributes. In the same vein, the entry of aversion excites each instrument to expose the negative attributes of the object of aversion and hide their positive attributes. The attachment (aversion) caused distortion of perception of the facts of reality render intelligence unstable.

Secondly, the selfish-will embodied ego also impels the over-shot actual level of attachment to generate the attachment-embodied (or non-neutral) thought contents of activity whose nucleus is selfish desires. In this way, greed and anger spring respectively from the realized and unrealized selfish desires to generate unbalanced inner self. The psychonomic perspective soaked in selfish desires generates (Verse 4-22) discontent, avarice, co-existence of contradictory tastes and psychic up and down swings. The unstable intelligence clouded by non-neutral thought contents (Verse 2-55) fails to inculcate the changeless which is the intrinsic nature of the Self. The impact of interaction between desires and work born of selfish-will also aggravates the impetuous nature of the senses (Verse 2-60 & 2-68) to unsettle intelligence, which is fostered by the impetuousness of the mind. The upshot of arguments noted above is that the inexorable and widespread restrictive impact of attachment-embodied thought contents of activity cause unbalanced inner self. This sets the stage for suboptimal use of the instruments contained in the domain.

Thirdly, the attachment-embodied thought contents of activity also destabilize the inner self by generating subjective (Chapter VI-3) constraints, making the psychic disposition (VI-4) highly sensitive to the ceaseless change occurring outside oneself.

Finally, the suboptimal use of the instruments contained in the domain is the consequence of constrained-concerns produced by the attachment-embodied thought contents of activity. The constrained-concerns conclude in constrained-activity. The phenomenon of constrained-activity is a byproduct of the interlaced nature of subjective constraints. The attachment to work in essence (Verse 6-4) is an outgrowth of attachment to self-indulgence through the senses. Even if one abstains from the act of self-indulgence (Verse 2-58 & 2-59) the long-lasting psychic impression of self-indulgence impels constrained action. The attachment to work and selfish desires exist at the same time with another. In principle, all human activities become a fact through the use of the instruments of activity as controlled by the triad of propensities. An individual's decision actualizes the use of the instruments as propelled by the obtaining composition of the thought currents of the triad of propensities. An individual is in full control of both the determinants of activity. The attachment manifests itself through its impact on (1) the self-sense of being a worker, (2) owner of the instruments contained in the domain, (3) attachment to work as evidenced by the impetus to work, and (4) return from work. The attachment to return from work is the axis (Verse 12-11) around which the subjective constraints arising from attachment to other aspects of work come up. The attachment to the entities both inside and outside the domain determines the extent or restrictive impact on the use of the instruments of activity. In other words the suboptimal use of the instruments contained in the domain becomes a fact because of attachment to people, work and its return. The attachment-embodied thought contents instigate constrained-concerns regarding (i) the self-sense of being a worker and (ii) the sense of being the rightful claimant of the return from work propelled by the urge to self-indulgence. The attachment to entities outside oneself tightly (Verse 4-22) interlocks the instruments of activity arresting their optimal functioning. The concern regarding completion of work and immediate return excites listlessness and lack of methodical execution of work. The self-sense of being a worker is an outgrowth of attachment to the instruments contained in the domain. The self-sense itself causes (Verse 18-59) suboptimal use of secondary human capital (the instruments of activity). The attachment to the self-sense of being a worker and to the instruments of activity provokes work motivated by selfish-will. As a result, the work itself internalizes attachment to bind egoism to the stream of active consciousness. This bind or subjective constraint in the first palace, binds the inner self by the relation between the urge to action and self-sense of being a worker hence diverts (Verse 3-27) concentration away from work. Secondly, the same subjective constraint deters the brightness of insight and foresight infused by the Self into intelligence.

The foregoing arguments demonstrate how the propensity to passion accommodated in ego brings about suboptimal use of the nature endowed instrument of activity contained in the domain. The same cause operative through the impulse of attachment and exaggerated self-sense of one's individuality results in suboptimal use of the primary human capital—that is, inputs provided by the Self. The overshooting of the actual level of attachment over its natural level (Chapter VI-1) provoked by the desires and work born of selfish-will, underlies the underutilization of the primary human capital. In the first place, the domain of activity propelled by the motives fixed in pleasure seeking, self-indulgence and selfishness emerges as the user of the total inputs endowed by nature and the Self. The diversion of the use of inputs by selfish-will to gratify the senses, gives rise to the tendency to curb the use of the inputs provided by the Self to exploit its intrinsic properties. Moreover, the impetus to work comes to be induced by selfish desires and attachment to work. Thus attachment-embodied thought contents strengthen the impetus to work. It is unnatural. This is for the reason that the necessary adjunct of such thought contents is impatience. This tendency suppresses the spontaneous flow of natural strength (Verse 7-11) sustained by patience as driven by the thought currents of purity.

Secondly, The Self being out of reach of nature and its creations is completely uninvolved (Verse 13-31 & 13-32) in whatever turns out in the domain of activity. Yet the Self bears the incidence (Chapter VI-4) of all shades of mental states thrown up by the domain. This is for the reason that all the occurrences materialize in the domain—that is, take place in the nature and by the nature. But the entities born of nature are devoid of consciousness—hence incapable to experience the ceaseless change. The self being the seat of consciousness is the preceptor (Verse 18-18) of all the preceptors lodged in the domain, called the senses. In case of non-appearance of overshooting of attachment, the Self ceases to experience psychic oscillations produced by the domain. In such a context the Self experiences non-neutral thought contents as which are fostered by the inputs provided by the Self.

Thirdly, human ego adapted to the propensity to passion steeps the domain into discompose. This is for the reason that the thought currents born of passion (Verse 14-12) cause disquiet within oneself. The non-realization of that is desired and or materialization of that is not desired gives rise to discontentment. The attachment to that is appealing and aversion to that is non-appealing provokes agitation induced by discontentment. The selfish-will born of passion is insatiable (Chapter V-2) and more so it envelops the brightness of wisdom in intelligence, aggravating discontent. The intelligence burdened with agitation (Verse 2-55) fails to identify the true source of contentment. The Self being beyond selfish-will is and everlasting source of contentment. The psychonomic perspective perpetually bombarded by selfish-will makes for short-lived recurring cycle of satisfaction and dissatisfaction. The true source of permanent contentment ceases to be realize because of wisdom eclipsed by attachment and aversion.

Finally, the suboptimal use of the instruments contained in the domain (secondary human capital) is upheld as the cause of failure to capitalize of the intrinsic properties of the Self. The intelligence established in the Self knows the difference between that is self-existent and non-existent, duty and non-duty and that is permanent and transient. This is the outcome of absolute knowledge. The ego enveloped by attachment and aversion tends to refract the currents of absolute knowledge from the medium of absolute consciousness the self to the medium of entities charged with devoid of consciousness. As a result the knowledge gained by the tools enlivened by the Self yields relative knowledge—subject to revision and revaluation. The relative knowledge acquired by the instruments of activity inside oneself is always imperfect. The struggles for perfection appear to be everlasting. As the overshot actual level of attachment (Verse 9-30) tends to zero, the decisions made by intelligence gets close and closer to the decision coming from the Self. The intelligence is said to be established in the Self.

Is it concluded that the perspective caused by passion adapted ego (Chapter VII) can be radically changed by the decision of an individual. The decision impelled by selfish motive concludes in the suboptimal use of the inputs provided by the Self and nature. This evidences the phenomena of underutilization of human capital.

*　*　*

CHAPTER-VII

THE MICRO APPROCH TO HUMAN WELFARE

It is put forward as a hypothesis that an individual can attain welfare for himself through work. The conclusions of the preceding chapters go a long way to deduce the rationale (Chapter VII-I) of welfare. We have noticed that work is generally used as a means to secure livelihood. For this reason the contribution of work to human life is a neglected issue. Work needs to be delivered from the bondage of selfish-will. It urges work to fulfill selfish desires by subduing will power. The emancipation from selfish-will is possible by altering the mode of use of the means available to and individual. The spirit of sacrifice and work done as sacrifice is upheld to negate the adverse impact of selfish-will. For this reason, the redemption of the domain of activity from attachment (Chapter VII-2) through work is the first step to attain welfare. We have seen else where (Chapter VI-2) that selfish-will internalizes attachment inside the domain. Therefore, some measures will have to be devised to minimize internalization of attachment (Chapter VII-3) inside the domain and maximize the flow of attachment (Chapter VII-4) outside the domain. These measures would impair the impact of selfish-will both on desires and work. The domain completely absolved of attachment also sets the stream of active consciousness free from non-neutral thought contents of activity. As a result, the retreat of the thought currents of passion and advance of the thought currents of purity (Chapter VII-5) establish the inner self in balanced disposition. The intelligence established in the Self grows capable to control the working of micro order. One established in the inner self is well disposed to work most efficiently. But an individual has to cultivate (Chapter VII-4) the art of working. It is needed to maintain the inner self in sustained balanced disposition. The essence of the art of working is devotion to work wholly unconstrained by attachment in any form whatsoever. These considerations show (Chapter VII-5) that the mode of the use of received inputs by the domain can improve and individual's welfare. An individual can engineer welfare for himself. This is followed by the test of welfare (Chapter VII-7) as an attainment of enduring contentment and peace.

VII-1 THE RATIONALE OF WELFARE

The lessons deduced from our imperfections also point out the direction for correction in future. We have seen earlier (Chapter-IV-5, Chapter-V & Chapter-VI) how the working of micro order, swayed by the thought currents of passion, impairs human welfare. The interactive impact of selfish-will and work done to carry it out, established selfish-will, as the prime mover of the micro order. The impulse of attachment and self-sense of one's individuality, born of passion, reinforce the modus operandi of selfish-will. The will power subdued by selfish-will degenerates into indeterminate horizon of indulgence in physical pleasures. The trajectory of life and livelihood comes to rotate around the bodily and worldly concerns. The compelling force of attachment casts an eclipse in varying degrees on the insight and foresight in the intelligence. Thus work is exclusively used as means to secure livelihood. This approach to work disregards the contribution of work to human life. Work used as a means to livelihood proxies for gratification of the senses through production, acquisition consumption and accumulation. Work is circumscribed by livelihood. Consequently, life of man, viewed as the state of existence, stands neglected.

Let us review the imperfections caused by the exclusive use of work as an instrument of livelihood. The imperfections essentially spring from the interactive impact of desires born of selfish-will and work accomplished to carry it out. The selfish-will, sheltered inside ego, enables it to diffuse its impact on the working of each component of the instrument of activity. Thus the push-out and pull-in of attachment, propelled by ego, concludes in large amount of flow of attachment inside the domain of activity. These trends give rise to spillover effects of significance. In the first place, it escalates the impetuous nature of the senses (Chapter-V-5) and mind which unsettles the state of intelligence. Secondly, the large amount of inflow of attachment in the domain of activity crystallizes (Chapter-VI-3 & VI-4) into a number of subjective constraints and regular cycle of joy and sorrow. The root cause of the discomposed working of the micro order dwells on the decision of individuals (Chapter-III-4) to use the available means for one's own welfare. The work prompted by selfish-will becomes inimical to work because it generates bondage to work. Work after its completion and its outcome after its consumption leaves a remainder of transient happiness. The natural functioning of micro order is disturbed by attachment to the self-sense of being and activity-achiever, attachment to the instruments of activity, impetus to work and its outcome. This context sufficiently proves that work actualizing one's own welfare impairs welfare. One continues to be pestered by indecision, doubts, conflicts, intrigues, stress and cycle of joy and sorrow.

The eventual conclusion of the review presented above indicates that exclusive concern for one's own welfare disturbs the natural functioning of the micro order. It implies that welfare can be secured through work by using the available means for the welfare of others without disregarding one's own welfare. Therefore, we contend that each individual can attain welfare, through performance of his own duty (Verse 18-46) towards others wholly untainted by selfish-will. The manifestations of selfish-will to people, objects of desire and work disrupts the functioning of the micro order. Therefore, we will demonstrate that abandonment of attachment would enable one to attain balanced disposition of the inner self, which is also the test of optimal efficiency in work. The balanced disposition of the inner self is a precondition for working with level-pegged mind unconstrained by selfish-will. The results of each step noted above, goes to establish the test of welfare. To foresee the end result, we submit that the thought and effort content of activity, uninfluenced by selfish-will, capitalizes on the inputs provided by nature, the Self and the order prevailing outside the domain of activity. The domain of activity is the final user of the received inputs. What matters most is the mode of use of the received inputs by the domain of activity. In other words, each individual is endowed with enough raw materials to secure enduring contentment, peace and happiness for himself.

VII-2 DELIVERY FROM THE BONDAGE TO WORK

Diagnosis precedes prescription. The cause of internalization of attachment inside oneself was identified (Chapter VI-2) to be the attachment-embodied (or non-neutral) thought contents of activity, operative both on the desire and work sides of human activity. It is evident that desire and work in their embryonic form appear as the thought contents of activity. The impulse called attachment binds individual's consciousness to desire and work. And the cyclical relation between the two set in motion the phenomena of internalization through impure personal nature. For this reason, the thought and effort contents of activity call for an incisive analysis to deliver oneself from internalization of attachment. An examination of the thought content of activity reveals the inner distinctive nature of work. The impulse of attachment creates bondage to work (Chapter VI-3, 4 & 5) and the work itself is premised to deliver oneself from the bondage. One can get rid of the bondage to work through work to attain welfare.

This contention appears to be unrealistic. This is for the reason that the nature born propensity to passion (Verse 14-7) is attachment incarnate. Moreover, the propensity is ingrained in human existence. Before we delve into the essence of work, it is necessary to disclose the role of the impulse of attachment as the 'relation-maker'. No activity is possible without the attachment—built relation of concern (Chapter II-5) between (i) the self and the instruments contained in the body, (ii) among the instruments themselves and (iii) between the instruments and the entities obtaining outside oneself. This spectrum of relations is natural and necessary. It is evident that no entity by it self can actualize any activity. We recall that the motives fixed in selfishness and self-indulgence (Chapter VI-1) induces overshooting of the actual level (intensity) of attachment over its natural level. Consequently, the relation-maker generates subjective constraints, psychic oscillations (Chapter VI-3, 4 & 5) and suboptimal use of the inputs provided by the Self and nature. But at the same time it is postulated that the relations built by attachment, likes and dislikes discerned by it and the urge to activity remain unimpaired (Verse 14-22) even if the actual level (intensity) of attachment is reduced to its natural level. This postulate provides a solid basis to deliver oneself from the restrictive impacts of internalized attachment.

The foregoing arguments set the stage to specify the essence of work. We contend that the listing of the essence of work would reveal the measures (Chapter VII-3) to set the domain of activity free from the restrictive impacts of internalization. It is postulated that (Verse 3-5) the impetus to work is timeless. This is because desires and work controlled by attachment sustain and escalate the impetus to work. The essence of work reveals how the actual level (intensity) of attachment can be reduced to its natural level to minimize the flow of attachment inside oneself and maximize its flow outside oneself. The essence of work (Verse 14-16) is listed as follows.

(1) The nomenclature of work is discerned by the thought content of activity underlying it. The desire, born of selfish-will, despite its being legitimate, incites indulgence in work to satisfy selfish motive. It is desire-embodied work. It is named as 'action'. The longing for the outcome of action is the prime mover of work. Now if the desire born of selfish-will incites action in illegitimate directions, it is called 'wrong action'. The phenomena of action, so also wrong action, being attachment-embodied, generate bondage to work. As compared to these two kinds of action, we have 'inaction'. In a generic sense, work born of attachment-disembodied thought content of activity delivers one from the bondage to work. For this reason, delivery from the bondage to work would necessitate to refrain from wrong action and gear action into inaction. The suggested measures must cause action to be untainted by attachment.

(2) The act of abstaining or indulgence in work both come to action. The urge to action either inclines or disinclines one to work. The essence of work consists in whether the disposition to work is, or not, driven by attachment. The impulse of attachment manifests itself as attachment to work, or immoderate sense of possession, or attachment to the outcome of work. In other words, one has to spell out whether the urge to abstain, or not to abstain, from work is attachment embodied, or disembodied. The attachment-embodied urge to action implies the concerned work would generate bondage to work. For this reason, the delivery from bondage to work necessitates an attitude of complete noninvolvement, or cultivating a tangential relation of concern before during and after the completion of work.

(3) The disposition of complete non involvement, even though one is engaged in work, is conditional upon the absence of bondage to work. The presence or absence of the bind respectively defines the true content of action and inaction. The bondage to work can be eliminated only by attainment (Chapter VII-4) of equanimity-or, balance inner self. It is the result of zero incidence of the impulse of attachment regardless of inclination or disinclination to work. It implies that the cause of bondage to work is not the effort, but the thought content of activity. The desire born of selfish will, immoderate the sense of possession and attachment to work generates bondage, regardless of one abstains, or does not abstain from work. The bondage to work is a subjective phenomenon. For this reason, the elimination of attachment from ego, intelligence and mind would scale down the actual level (intensity) of attachment to its natural level.

(4) The essence of work is based on the premise that work itself eliminates the bondage to work. In the first place, it is established that the bondage to work comes into existence because of the saturation of the thought content of activity with attachment. The causative factor of bondage is the attachment-embodied thought content of activity. The effort content of activity is machine like-action without thought. Secondly, although the urge to activity and the impulse of attachment-both are born of the propensity to passion, the urge to activity (Verse 14-22) is independent of attachment. These two aspects taken together reflect upon the nature of required work. It has to deflect the incidence of impulse of attachment from inside to outside oneself. To be precise the work has to generate unconcern (detachment) inside oneself and concern (attachment) to execute work outside oneself. It implies that the means available to and individual must be used (Chapter III-3) for the betterment of others without disregarding (Verse 3-8) once own self-interest. We can create the perspective of 'unconstrained-concern'. It is inactivation of attachment inside oneself but 'concerned-concern' to conclude the entire sequence of work outside oneself.

These aspects of the essence of work indicate the basis for minimizing the process of internalization of attachment. The outline of the suggested measures are intended (i) to set one free from selfish desires and (ii) oriented to benefit others driven by the motive of selfless service and sacrifice.

VII-3 EXTERNALISATION OF ATTACHMENT

The essence of work (Chapter VII-2) provides the basis for a systemic approach to deliver the domain of activity from the impact of internalized attachment. The set of measures be so designed as to minimize the flow of attachment inside oneself, along with maximizing its flow outside one self. It is contended that the flow of attachment in the desired directions can be actualized though work. As such the issue is how and individual can bring about a net flow of attachment outside oneself on the basis of the four-pronged essence of work. An individual can be viewed as the hub of relations of concern with respect to people, goods and services and work (action). This is for the reason that no one is self-sufficient. A network of dependences sustains and individual's life and livelihood. The objective of externalization of attachment is attainable through radical change in the attitude to work. It is contended that work can be used as a device to strip off attachment from the network of the relations of concern in force. The conclusion of the preceding section requires and individual to cultivate unconstrained-concern inside oneself, at the same time carry out work with concerned—concern. It means, in the first place that an individual's decision and the operation of each instrument, contained in the body, must not be constrained by attachment. Secondly, while executing the work the actual level (intensity) of attachment ought not be permitted to overshoot its natural level. It is postulated that (Verse 18-45) one committed to work as duty can attain perfection. Individuals will have to undertake work in the spirit of duty the commitment of duly is the correct attitude to accept work. The terms work as duty refers to forgo (Verse 3-19) the valued selfish interest, for the sake of higher consideration of betterment of others, keeping due regard to one's own capacity and regards for self Interest. The network of relations, both inside and outside the family, and ever changing circumstances signal an opprtunity and obligation to act.

The attitude of commitment to work as duty peels off attachment in the present inside oneself, as well as provides an ideal psychic state to carry out work. The eyes centered upon work as duty causes one to be unconstrained by attachment to its anticipated return, belongingness of the instruments contained in the body, one's own capacity and the self-sense of being a worker. And the sacrifice of longing for the return from work effaces the incidence of attachment in future. The incidence of attachment obscures the rational commitment to take up work as duty. The devotion to duty requires one (i) to be regardless of one's own rights (ii) but be regardful of one's own duty and (iii) be unmindful of the duty of others. The spirit of duty obliges one to render selfless service to others, without expecting anything in exchange. The following rules (Verse 3-10, 11 & 12) operationalize the spirit of work as duty, both with and without reference to a particular person. We propose to consider the issue with reference one working to serve a person or set of persons. In the first place, variety of instruments contained in the body and endowment of insight and foresight empowers man with capacity to work. One can use these inputs to achieve the best possible outcome from each favorable and unfavorable circumstance. Secondly, the performance of duty by each and every individuals consistent with the requirement of others members of the family, so also assignments allotted by vocation, approximates to one serving every one separately and every one separately serving one. It implies that the total benefits accruing to one would be equal to the aggregate contributions of many. It implies that the concern of oneself cannot be divorced from the concerns of other selves. This approach to work as duty ensures ceaseless supply of work-materials and consumables to every one. Finally, it is also advocated that whatever is received from others must be used to serve others (Verse 3-12), without detaining even a fraction of it to satisfy selfish-will. The act of withholding that is received from others amounts to leakage—that is, scaling down the existing aggregate level (Verse 3-15, 16) of the circular order sustaining life and livelihood, of every individual.

Thus far we have considered by operationalization of work as duty by one serving a person or a set of persons. Now we reconsider the same issue without such references. The operationalization of work in the two cases is respectively labeled as 'service' and 'sacrifice'. The spirit and contents of service and sacrifice both demand to forgo something valued for the sake of something higher. The act of sacrifice is not an exchange of something valued lower for something valued higher. In fact something valued has to be outright given up. Consequently, as the incidence of something valued lower tends into insignificance, something higher spontaneously takes its place. The desire and work impelled by selfish will has to be given up. The selfish-will incites internationalization (chapter VI) of attachment. It is the cause of bondage to work. Therefore, attachment has to be stripped off from desires, self-sense of being a worker, belongingness of instruments, contained in the body, one's own capacity and outcome of work. The removal of the attachment-embodied thought content of activity not only discontinues internationalization of attachment, but also prepares the groundwork for inaction—work unconstrained by the bondage to work. Accordingly, the act of sacrifices In no way implies abandonment of people, goods and services and work indispensable to sustain the detaining network of relations of concern. The real content of sacrifice demands (Verse 5-12 and 18-9) to turn away from attachment within oneself from outcome of work, selfish-will and seeking pleasure in work, even though one is engaged in work as duty. For this reason, the essence of contribution of sacrifice to welfare does not depend upon work, but in disembodying work from attachment in every respect.

Now while the spirit of sacrifice is inestimable, sacrifice in concrete terms is enclosed within the bounds of available resources. But the unwillingness and willingness to sacrifice respectively reflect the cost and benefit of sacrifice. Until the cost of sacrifice is less, or at least equal to the benefit of sacrifice, the spirit of sacrifice would die out. The cost of sacrifice is evidenced by the resistance to be separated from the pleasure derived from the gratification of the senses. This is passion incited happiness. It is of a lower order (Verse 18-36 & 37) as compared to the happiness untainted by passion. The work accomplished as duty stimulates the spirit of sacrifice as provoked by (Verse 18-37) the happiness of purity. For this reason, the accrual of happiness of higher order offsets or more than offsets, the unwillingness to sacrifice. The effectiveness of the spirit of sacrifices depends upon (i) the urge to render selfless service to others and (ii) the brightness of wisdom unobscured by attachment, in intelligence. The intensity of the urge to selfless service enhances the capacity to forgo the longing for consumption and leisure. The unobscured wisdom infuses the spirit of changelessness— that is, generates a tendency to turn away from desire and work born of selfish-will hence keep eyes fixed on the end result of work. One comes to realize that work after its completion and outcome after its consumption becomes non-existent, leaving a remainder of unfinished portfolio of desire and work. As against this, work as duty sustained by the spirit of sacrifice and delight of intelligence (Chapter VII-4) leaves behind a remainder of equanimity—lasting balanced disposition of one's own inner self.

VII-4 THE BALANCED INNER SELF

It is postulated that individuals can attain welfare (Verse 3-11) is a supreme sense by undertaking work (Verse 3-9) as and for sacrifice. The attitude of work as duty is the co-operant of sacrificial work. The preceding sections (Chapter VII-2 & VII-3) demonstrate how the bind imposed by work can be unfastened through work itself. The spirit of sacrifice propels the selfish desire disembodied work as duty for the betterment of others, without (Verse 3-8) disregarding one's own. The text of the suggested approach not only minimizes the flow of attachment inside oneself and maximizes the flow of attachment outside oneself but also requires to cultivate the sameness of attributes between one's own inner self and the Self. It is signifies that the destination of work and its outcome is other than oneself. This raises the issue of gain accruing to a worker as the remainder of work. The basis for further discussion (Verse 4-31) is that the selfish desire disembodied work for the betterment of others leaves behind a remainder that carries the attributes of nectar. The remainder accrues in two distinct stages. The remainder of sacrificial work becomes noticeable at first in one's own (Verse 2-48) inner self— that is, ego, intelligence and mind. To be precise, the remainder as the balanced inner self as the first manifestation of itself matures into the higher yield of the remainder. In other words, the balanced inner self grows up into 'supreme welfare'. The term supreme is indicative of the sameness of attributes between the alive entity (the Self) and inner self, or the non-alive entities (instruments of activity contained in the body). The balanced inner self advances in degrees to yield the sameness of aattributes between the entity endowed with consciousness, knowledge, insight, foresight and entities devoid of consciousness. Thus the remainder of sacrifical work requires to expose (1) the nature of the remainder, (2) how does it build the inner self of an individual and (3) the consequences of the accumulated remainder.

We start to examine the nature of the balanced inner self first. The human ego, intelligence and mind, or the internal instruments of activity, constitute the inner self. The term balance is indicative of complete absence of tilting of the 'pan' on either side of the "physical balance". This is an inapt analogy. This is for the reason that, the lack of tilting on either side could be due to (a) equal weights on both the pans, or (b) no weights on either of the pans. We prefer to explain the term balance as an absence of attachment and aversion on both the pans.

The intelligence positioned mid-way between ego and mind is the fulcrum of the balanced inner self. This is for the reason that the impetuous nature of ego and the senses through the mind (Chapter V-4) upset the balanced state of intelligence. The radical change in decision evoked by sacrifice and reinforced by selfless service impairs the restrictive and rigid impact of ego. As a result—'ego adapted to radical change in decision (Chapter III-3) triggers an advance of the thought currents of purity and retreat of the thought currents of passion.

The release of the seize of the propensity to passion on ego removes its destablising influence on intelligence. The externalization of the impulse of attachment (Chapter Vll-3) outside the domain of activity, or oneself, impairs the second destabiling influence on intelligence.

The second destabilizer is the impetuous nature of the senses. It forcibly draws mind on its side (Verse 2-60) to throw intelligence out of balance. The intelligence set free from the entities controlled by attachment and self-centeredness unrolls the attributes unclouded by attachment and egoism. It tends to become unchangeable, resolute, free from self-contradictions and tends to be self-possessed. The degree of steadiness in intelligence is the indicator of the extent of balanced inner self.

The next issue is how balanced inner self grows through the steadiness of intelligence. It is a fact of ultimate reality that intelligence is the receiver of the inputs supplied by the Self (Chapter II-4) through ego in the micro order. Therefore, the contents of the inputs supplied by the self-existent entity (the Self) are also self-existent. The attributes of these inputs are unshake-ability (stable and well-foundedness) and immobility (settled, rational and unchangeable). Accordingly, human intelligence is essentially steady and rational. But ego lies in the middle of the transmission of inputs from the Self to intelligence. Consequently, the natural (or alive) counterpart of ego (Chapter II-3) urged by attachment to body and gratification of the senses adds large weightage to comfort and leisure. As such the decisions made by intelligence are to a large extent precepted by ego. The rationale of sacrificial work, capitalizes on the above noted fact of reality. It scales down the actual level of attachment and self-centeredness to its natural level to restore the steadiness of intelligence. In other words, as the restrictive impacts of attachment and egoism decreases, the increasing assimilation of inputs supplied by the Self through intelligence causes the initial stage of balanced, inner self to mature into the higher stage. This is the acid test of settled intelligence. As such intelligence is said to be established in the Self. In what follows we outline a few kinds of sacrificial work which build the intrinsic qualities of the Self into the domain of activity through intelligence. The attributes of intelligence tend to acquire (Verse 14-2) sameness with the Self.

In the first instance sacrificial works necessitate; a radical change in the attitude of individuals. This is necessary to keep the achieved balanced inner self going over time. In general, the assumption of being a work-achiever stimulates attachment to the outcome of work and the two together gives rise to attachment to work-material. The fact of reality is that (Verse 4-24) the macro order is both the supplier and user of variety of inputs, non-human capital and human capital. At the same time the macro order is also the producer and consumer of the produced products. The acceptance of the noted fact of reality entrusts an obligation on individuals. Each individual must strive for unconstrained-concern on the desire and work sides of activity. The commitment to work *as* duty makes the objectives of the macro and micro order consistent. In other words, the thought content of activity underlying consumption and work must be free from each and every manifestation of attachment. The owner of work-material becomes its holder and manager of the inputs received from the Self, nature and macro order (Chapter Vll-6) in an optimal manner. Consequently, the impulse of attachment and selfish-will flows out of oneself, through the spirit and work done for the betterment of others.

Another direction of sacrificial work to maintain the achieved balanced inner self is disciplining (Verse 4-26)—of the senses. It is postulated that (1) each instrument, contained in the body, must be cleansed of the restrictive impact of attachment and (2) the employment of the senses for self-indulgence, through their respective objects, must not change the posture (agitate) of the senses. It is noticeable that each of the instruments of activity, untainted by selfish-will, naturally causes the act of self-indulgence to generate the contentment of purity rather than pleasure-seeking incited by passion. The sacrifice in terms of the withdrawal of the senses (Verse 2-58) from their respective objects, together with devotion to work as duty depends upon the decision of an individual. The spirit and pursuit of selfish desire-disembodied work for the betterment of others, causes the natural (or alive) counterpart of ego to turn away (Chapter III-3) from the gratification of the senses and accumulation of wealth. As a result the changed perspective tends to replace the ego-led perspective in discreet steps by a new order. Consequently, as the use of inputs provided by the Self is increasingly used for sacrificial work, the new perspective comes into being. The end result is brightening of the intrinsic qualities of the Self, unconstrained by ego, into intelligence. This is for the reason that the emergence of egolessness itself restrains internalization of attachment and encourages its externalization outside oneself. The extent of disclosure of the Self in intelligence depends upon (a) the degree upto which sacrificial work weakens (Verse 2-55) the incidence of desire born of selfish—will and (b) impairs (Verse 3-27) the self-sense of being a worker. In fact, the impact of sacrificial work simultaneously undermines desire born of selfish-will and work induced by selfish-will. The resulting perception of steadiness in intelligence, truly speaking, is a reflection of the self-existent entity— the Self.

The state of egolessness caused by selfless service and sacrificial work is a highly important phenomenon. It drastically scales down the inclination towards self-indulgence and accumulation of wealth. This tendency weakens the strength of acquired ego. This is same thing as the removal of ego-curtain between the Self and intelligence. Consequently, the incidence of inputs supplied by the Self (Verse 6-5) percolates through each instrument contained in the body, unpolluted by attachment and aversion. The authority of the Self comes to precept the working of the domain of activity. The thought currents of illumination and knowledge efface the destabilizing influences on the working of the instruments contained in the body. In other words, the thought currents of purity act as the cause-way between the self and intelligence. As a result the decisions made by intelligence (Verse 9-30) increasingly grow consistent with insight and foresight emitted by the Self. The steadiness of intelligence becomes an independent variable (Verse 18-33) to regulate the working of the senses through the mind. The onset of absolute knowledge in intelligence (caused by egolessness) accelerates the move towards the balanced inner self, which generates optimal skill (Verse 2-50) to execute work, hence produces the conditions to cultivate (Chapter VII-5) the art of working.

The steady-state intelligence, as the cause and consequence of the remainder of sacrificial work, spills over into other repercussions of equal significance. This is for reason of the advance of the thought currents of purity and retreat of the thought currents of passion. The attained steadiness of intelligence operates through an increasingly increasing influence of wisdom, along with increasingly decreasing influence of attachment and egoism. Both these tendencies affect the working of each instrument contained in the body. Consequently, the thought currents of illumination cause optimal working of the each instrument of activity. This is because of the decreasing impact of attachment and aversion restores (Verse 18-45) the spontaneous working of the micro order. The thought currents of knowledge, born of purity, gather strength to shift the entire psychic disposition of and individual from change to changelessness. That is to say, all relations of concern born of attachment increasingly give way to those precepted by wisdom. In other words, the network of constrained—concerns grow into unconstrained-concerns. The knowledge gained from ceaseless change—through the relation between the instruments of activity and the outside world, increasingly give more weight age to knowledge derived by the same instruments of activity from the changeless Self through intelligence. The detachment from the attachment—caused concerns and attachment to wisdom precepted concerns generates two significant effects.

Finally we propose to consider the consequences of the attained balanced inner self. The steady-state intelligence, as the cause and consequence of the remainder of sacrificial work, spills over into other repercussions of equal significance. This is for reason of an advance of the thought currents of purity and retreat of the thought currents of passion. Thus the steady-state of intelligence operates through an increasingly increasing influence of wisdom—insight and foresight, along with increasingly decreasing influence of attachment and egoism. Both these tendencies affect the working of each instrument contained in the body. Consequently, the abetment of attachment (and its obverse aversion) and strengthening of wisdom in intelligence generates the perspective of egelessness. For this reason, the egoless perspective makes (1) the subjective constraints, irrespective of their origin, ineffective and (2) wipes out the tendency of psychic oscillations—that is, compelling deviations from the balanced inner self.

Let us consider the nature of the egoless perspective first. We recall that selfish desire-disembodied work done for the betterment of others describes the essence of sacrificial work. The sacrificial work is a powerful device to arrest internalization of attachment and quicken its externalization. It is noticeable that neither the Self, nor the instruments contained in the body shelter attachment in any form whatsoever. As a result they remain unmoved by the net flow of attachment outside oneself. But ego because of its peculiar constitution (Chapter II-3) is emptied of its strength. This is for the reason that ego accommodates attachment to one's own body, instruments contained in the body and entities obtaining outside oneself. In fact, all the entities other than the Self are devoid of consciousness. And activity is action without thought. The impulse of attachment in essence, seizes all non-alive entities. The sacrificial work is a powerful tool to cleanse attachment from ego through escalating the flow of work and its outcome for the betterment of others. The inner self is set free from the rule of attachment and aversion. As such, all kinds of concerns constrained by attachment become unconstrained—concerns. Accordingly the human ego as the agent of conscious activity ceases to propel work induced by selfish-will. This phenomenon is one facet of egolessness. The other facet of egolessness is the rise of the Self out of the eclipse imposed by ego as the principle of life.

The first impact of egolessness is evidenced by an elimination of the subjective constraints, born of an interaction between egoism and attachment. The subjective constraint originate (Verse 4-37) because of (a) accumulation of attachment in past periods due to selfish-will induced work and (b) selfish desire-embodied work carried out in the present period. The subjective constraints caused by accumulation of attachment in past periods conceive because of selfish desires. It fosters ignorance by obscuring the brightness of wisdom in intelligence. However, in the egoless state the rise of the Self dispels the attachment-caused indistinctness on wisdom. The insight and foresight originating in the Self prevail over the attachment (aversion) in decision making. The impulse of reason dispels all kinds of constrained-concerns sustained by attachment. The size of the portfolio of selfish desires shrinks because of (Chapter V-2) the awareness of its end result. The subjective constraints originating in attachment to work, executed in the present period, also meets their end because of the non-appearance of attachment to the outcome of work. The egolessness, in fact, impairs the attachment to fruit of work, because one ceases to be motivated by the self-sense of being a worker. Briefly speaking, the engagement in work, without attachment to its outcome (Verse 12-11) subsides the impetus to action and the attachment accumulated in past periods. The absence of longing for the outcome of work eliminates attachment to work and arrests the rise of attachment in new directions.

The perspective of egolessness is also evidenced by cessation of the deviations of the psychic state from the balanced inner self. The omission of shakability of the inner self is the result of the combined impact of both the facets of egolessness. The externalization of attachment induced by sacrificial work and the increasing influence of the Self on the instruments of activity, builds unconstrained-concerns in the entire network of relations of concern. These tendencies minimize the frequency of occurrence of psychic swing (Verse 5-26), reduce its intensity and the duration of its stay in the psychonomic perspective. To be precise, the externalization of attachment outside the domain of activity makes two primary causes of psychic swings ineffective. In the first place, the self-sense of one's individuality and the pride of belongings are deleted as selfish-will ceases to neutralize one's own will power. Secondly, the sacrificial work extinguishes the motive fixed in pleasure seeking through self-indulgence and wipes out psychic swings causes by success and failures. This is for the reason that an individual uses the total of received inputs from all sources for the betterment of others rather than of one's own self. This aspect of externalization raises a serious issue. One indifferent to gratification of the senses and immune from the manifestations of success (failures) would lose all concerns in life and livelihood. This is not so. The retreat of the propensity to passion and advance of the propensity to purity in the psychonomic perspective increasingly fosters the assimilation of the inputs provided by the Self into each instrument of activity thought intelligence. Consequently, one turns away from the transient sources of pleasure to permanent longing for contentment, knowledge and reason to rise above the whirl of change. The psychonomic perspective is transported to a higher plane which yields most objective awareness of circumstances and incites apt measures to achieve the best possible results out of the favorable and unfavorable circumstances, but does not generate psychic swings.

VII-5 THE ART OF WORKING

It is postulated that one established in the balanced inner self is also well-founded in work culture. This is the route to attain welfare. It implies that the attained balanced inner self is a necessary, but not sufficient condition to achieve welfare. This is for the reason that an individual has to cultivate the art of non-involvement in work. It saves one from the pitfall or selfish-will. The selfish will arrests the achievement of the balanced inner self and makes one opaque to the art of working. Therefore the presence of two-way causation between the balanced inner self and complete non-involvement in work must be exploited. The cultivation of complete non-involvement in work concludes in the balanced inner self.

As a prelude to subsequent arguments the connotation of work and the basis of skill of executing work is spelt out. The act of indulgence (doing) and abstaining from (not doing) work are the two facets of the same coin, called work. The notion of work is inclusive of indulgence in and abstaining from work as duty. The essential feature of the art of working consists in transforming personalized concerns into impersonal concerns for work. The personalization of work should be impersonalized. This constitutes the basis (Verse 2-50) for carrying out work. Personalization embodying selfishness and pride of being a worker internalizes attachment. It besets the working of the instruments of activity contained in the domain with (Chapter VI-3) subjective constraints. The personal considerations in performance of work involve one in complicated circumstances. The concern with work comes to be constrained by personal considerations. The work is seized by the phenomena of 'constrained-concern'. Accordingly, the total removal of personal considerations would impersonalize work. This measure would occasion complete non-involvement in work. Consequently, the natural functioning of the instruments contained in the domain will be restored (Verse 18-45) as work would be stripped off attachment and aversion incited by personal considerations. The complete non-involvement in work, exempt from personal considerations, would yield optimal results. To be precise, the essence of complete non-involvement in work requires one to develop an objective attitude to work. The Self despite being a conscious entity is completely non-involved in work. One has to foster sameness with the innate quality of the Self. The personalization of work coats the relation of concern with complete involvement. For this reason, the elimination of the personal considerations would not only ensure (i) natural functioning of the instruments contained in the domain, but also cause (ii) the inner self to develop sameness with the Self. The attainment of likeness between the Self and the inner self brightens insight and foresight in intelligence. One comes to realize that the outcome of work after its consumption leaves nothing as a remainder. For this reason, the inner self gradually turns away from change (transient) to changelessness (something enduring). One grows detached from personal considerations, or grows completely non-involved in work. The arts of working reveal the substance of work on the condition that the inner self is inextricably unconcerned with work while working or not working. The concern ought not to be tainted by the attachment-embodied (non-neutral) thought contents of activity. The unconstrained concern with work concludes in the art of working.

The problem is how the inner self be anchored in complete non-involvement in work. The act of indulging in and abstaining from work both describe the effort content of work. The effort content amount to action without thought. It lacks the capacity to induce involvement or non-involvement. For this reason, the quality of thought, as the mainspring of effort, conceals the cause of involvement (Verse 4-16), or non-involvement in work. It is axiomatic that each manifestation of attachment while indulging in or abstaining from work necessarily closes in complete involvement in work. The impulse of attachment hatches selfish-will which personalizes work, (Chapter VI-2) through non-neutral thought contents of activity. Thus the disclosure of selfish-will in the form of attachment to achieved ends, longing for unachieved ends and attachment to work evidences complete involvement in work. It denotes engagement either as indulgence in or abstaining from work. As against this, one delivered from selfish-will is completely non-involved in work. The sign of complete non-involvement is an absence (Verse 3-17) of the self-sense of being a worker, even though one is fully engaged in work. In means that the absence of selfish-will keeps the balanced inner self intact, hence unconstrained engagement in work. Briefly speaking, non-neutral thought contents explain the essence of unconcerned-concern with work. The unconstrained-concern firmly fixes one in the state of complete non-involvement in work.

A more important issue is the operationalization of the notion of complete non-involvement in work. The unvarying engagement prescribes two rules (Verse 4-18) to take for complete non-involvement in work. The rule—I requires one to maintain equilibrium (complete non-involvement) while "doing" or abstaining from work. The rule-II requires one to be established in equilibrium (complete non-involvement) "before" indulging in or abstaining from work. Let us consider the rule-I first. In principle the longing for the return from work (Verse 4-14) ends in bondage to work. For this reason, while executing work one ought not be moved by early and easy completion of work, longing for its return and gain in prestige and status. Similarly, abstaining from work ought not be motivated by public acclamation arising out of self-denial, comfort and leisure of threat of toil in working. The logic of non-involvement is that neither indulging in nor abstaining from work be self-serving. Work instigated by selfish-will has to be abandoned. The bind of attachment in new directions ceases to be effective when one gives up selfish-will. And unselfish performance of work for the benefit of others erases attachment accumulated in past periods. The logical basis of these arguments is that an omission of selfish-will on the side of desires and work spontaneously helps to bring about complete non-involvement in work.

The rule-II requires one to be established in complete non-involvement before indulging in or abstaining from work. The logical basis of the rule is than one, like the Self (Verse 13-31) should remain untainted by attachment to work and its outcome. The implication being that all bodily and worldly concerns are meant for entities other than the Self. The attitude of even-mindedness in work draws one closer to the Self. The ultimate purpose of work is (Verse 3-20) to build the infrastructure of attitude for exploitation and accumulation of human capital. The rule-II is actualized through sacrificial work. The objective of sacrificial work (Chapter V11-3) is to eliminate the thought contents of activity arising from attachment to entities devoid of consciousness and exploit the absolute knowledge through the use of life energy infused by the Self. In other words, the intrinsic properties of the Self have to be fully exploited to facilitate the management of the entities devoid of consciousness as inputs. The absolute non-appearance of selfish-will makes the objective of sacrificial work a fact. One grows completely non-involved in work (Verse 3-18) as one has nothing to gain either from indulging in or abstaining from work. Sacrificial work establishes one completely in the context of selflessness.

One last observation is in order about the rationale of the balanced inner self (Chapter VII-3) and complete non-involvement in work. The art of working brings about complete non-involvement and balanced inner self to reinforce each other. Consequently, one gets hold on (i) the enduring balanced inner self for his own self and (ii) accomplish work for others. The former gain firmly fixes an individual in the self-earned norm of welfare. These consequences also underwrite freedom from psychic oscillations (Chapter VI-4) arising from completion or non-completion of work and or receipt or non-receipt of the desired outcome from work.

This is for the reason that the balanced inner self reveals (Verse 5-20) the most objective awareness of the facts of reality and discloses apt action to meet reality without causing psychic oscillations. The awareness and knowledge made available by the inner self is always free from imperfections. The imperfections arise due to selfish-will which generates the self-sense of being a worker and longing for the outcome of work. In the changed context the attitude fixed upon work (Verse 2-56 & 2-57) makes one immune from the generally observed reactions caused by non-appealing behavior (Verse 6-9) of people, changes in the achieved stock (Verse 6-8) of material and immaterial sources of pleasure. The psychonomic perspective is also emancipated from subjective constraints of different origin.

VII-6 THE EXPLOITATION OF HUMAN CAPITAL

Individuals are endowed with a unique assortment of inputs provided by the Self and nature. The world outside oneself also provides individuals with a variety of inputs. The term input denotes anything taken-in by the system of production, exchange, consumption and accumulation. It is hypothesized that the optimal use of nature endowed inputs by the domain leads to full utilization of human capital. In support of this premise we contend that the world may provide with an ever increasing size, quality and composition of inputs in the form of skill and technology, but man survives as its ultimate user. For this reason, even at the cost of repetition, we suggest that the instruments contained in the domain of activity denote secondary human capital and is animator (Chapter II-5)—that is, the Self as the primary human capital. For this reason, the full utilization of human capital depends upon the 'mode' of use of the received inputs from the Self and nature by the domain. Consequently, we concluded earlier (Chapter VI-5) that the decision motivated by selfishness fixes the mode of use of the received inputs by the domain. In the present context we premise that the decision impelled by unselfish motive controls the mode of use of the received inputs by the domain.

The decision incited by selfish motive causes the use of the received inputs exclusively for self-indulgence and accumulation of wealth. As such, desire and work propelled by selfish-will restricts the issue of human welfare to earning of livelihood—the outer self of man. This approach neglects the contribution of work to human life and welfare—the inner self of man. The overemphasis on livelihood is beset with subjective (Chapter VI-3) constraints and psychic (Chapter VI-4) oscillations closing in an unbalanced inner self. The unbalanced inner self (Chapter VII-4) is neither conducive to exploitation of the potentialities of the Self, nor the optimal use of the inputs provided by nature. The obtaining state of affairs impairs human welfare despite increasing contribution of prosperity. The never ending search for balanced inner self coexists with the ever expanding frontiers of affluence.

In view of the foregoing arguments now we proceed to consider how the mode of use of inputs by the domain, driven by unselfish motive, ensures full utilization of the primary and secondary human capital. It is premised that full utilization of secondary human capital—that is, optimal use of the instruments contained in the domain spontaneously lead to full utilization of the primary human capital. The constitution of the micro order tells us that any change in the composition of ego affects the Self, ranked above it, and as well as the instruments contained in the domain ranked lower than it. And that (ii) the stream of active consciousness reflects the changes caused by any of the four independent variables influencing the micro order. The changed composition of ego and corresponding placement of the thought currents of purity, passion and passivity in the stream of active consciousness is made possible by (Chapter III-3) the decision of individuals driven by unselfish motive. It implies that the natural working of the instruments contained in the domain (Verse 18-45) is possible only when ego is cleansed of the attachment-embodied thought contents of activity, generated by the propensity of passion and passivity. These thought contents of activity can be deleted by (1) restraining the flow of attachment (Chapter VII-2) inside oneself and (2) accelerating the flow of attachment (Chapter VII-3) outside oneself. The work acts as a double edged weapon (Chapter VII-5) to set off a large net flow of attachment outside oneself. The sacrificial work done to benefit others without disregarding (Verse 3-8) one's own needs and wishes absolves each (i) instrument from the incidence of attachment and aversion and (ii) enables one to be established in poise even though one is engaged (Verse 2-64 & 2-65) in self-indulgence.

The attainment of both these objectives in principle depends upon (i) getting rid of egoism, (ii) discouraging the flow of attachment inside oneself and (iii) encouraging the flow of attachment outside oneself. Now since the thought content of activity is the determinant of its effort content, the quality of thought contents of activity matter most in the full utilization of the secondary human capital. For this reason, the text suggests (Verse 13-11) strict adherence to the norms of knowledge and avoid the pitfall of non-knowledge. The putting of knowledge into practice causes ego-lessness and decelerates the flow of attachment inside oneself. And disregarding non-knowledge accelerates the flow of attachment and egoism outside oneself. It is noteworthy that the combined effect of executing the norms of knowledge and non-knowledge intensifies (Chapter V-3) the weight of neutral as compared to non-neutral thought contents of activity in the thought portfolio. The relative weights of these thought contents eliminate the constraints imposed by egoism and attachment, hence conducive to optimal working of the instruments contained in the domain. To be precise, the occurrence of these changes in the input-mix and output-mix (Chapter III-5 & IV-4) of the instruments contained in the domain not only affect the secondary but the primary human capital as well, to end in full utilization of both. This is another way of stating full utilization of the secondary human capital. The non-neutral thought contents of activity originating from non-knowledge are (Verse 16-4) covetousness, violence, harshness, excessive pride, anger, malice, ignorance and fault finding. the neutral thought contents of activity born of knowledge are absence of pride, steadfastness, self control (Verse 13-7), indifference to the objects of sense, self-effacement, perception of all that agitates mind and abandoning attachment and motives fixed in (Verse 13-9) selfishness and embracing (Verse 13-9) that is self-existent and everlasting. The repercussions to strict adherence to knowledge and non-knowledge strengthen one's will power through erosion of selfish-will. This erosion helps (i) to deliver the instruments of activity from attachment (Chapter VII-4) and aversion, without disturbing one established in balanced inner self and (ii) maintains poise while satisfying personal inclinations which awakens (Verse 2-64 & 2-65) delight in intelligence.

The preceding arguments imply that the stream of active consciousness (Chapter III-3) now embodies the thought currents of purity in its upper segment, carrying more or equal strength as the thought currents of passion; hence the thought currents of passivity recede in the lower segment of the stream. The changed propensity-mix also induces a change in the composition of ego. Consequently, the natural ego uneclipsed by acquired ego gathers strength for the reason that the actual level (or intensity) of attachment and egoism collapse to their natural level. This tendency is fostered by the growing strength of the thought currents of purity. As a result, attachment-disembodied work and absence of craving from the return from work reduces the current impetus to work. And the non-appearance of attachment to work desists the rise of new impetus to work. The impulse of attachment turned away from inside oneself makes the instruments of activity free from attachment and aversion; hence generate non-involvement in work even though one is working. These tendencies intensify spontaneous working (Verse 18-45) of the micro order. Yet another impact of the changed propensity-mix is that the stream of active consciousness saturated with the thought currents of purity enlightens every instrument of activity which now operates unconstrained by the impulse of attachment and egoism. The secondary human capital or the instruments contained in the domain stands utilized to its full capacity—that too all spontaneously.

The rise in the strength of natural ego and upsurge of the thought currents of purity awaken brightness of insight and foresight in intelligence. We recall that the stream of active consciousness and wisdom as being the product of a self-existent entity the Self, are also (Verse 18-16) self-existent. It implies that the thought currents of purity mediate between the Self and the intelligence to transfuse the trends which escalate full utilization of the primary human capital. In other words, the obtaining conditions of changed composition of the propensity-mix and ego not only account for full utilization of the secondary human capital, but also responsible for the exploitation of the intrinsic qualities of the Self. As the assimilation of the qualities of the Self in intelligence, unconstrained by attachment and egoism, gathers strength (Verse 5-20 & 9-30) to produce neutral thought contents of activity the intelligences gets established in the Self and conquers the domain of activity. This is the acid test of full utilization of the primary and secondary human capital.

VII-7 THE TEST OF WELFARE

Now we bring up the logical sequence and the test of the attained welfare. We contend that and individual can attain welfare all by him himself through work. The art of working at the micro level supplements the contributions of the macro order to the life and livelihood of individuals. The accepted manifestations of welfare are delight, contentment and satisfaction arising from the relationship with kins, consumption of food (Verse 3-17) and accumulation of wealth. These objects of desire are perishable, or transient, in nature, hence the resulting welfare, indexed by an ordinal measure of utility, is necessarily short-lived. The nature of gain in utility keeps the urge to acquire, consume and accumulate compelling over the whole life span. In fact, our eagerness for an object, is proportional to the intensity of attachment for the object, hence gain in utility is proportional to the extent of attachment. To repeat, the cause of utility is likeability and likeability is a consequence of attachment. This line of reasoning suggests, in principle, that gain in utility is proportional to the intensity of attachment. Therefore, it axiomatically follows that attachment to perishable objects yields short-lived utility. For that reason, the absence of craving for perishable objects yields contentment. Each perishable object carries some property to yield satisfaction. But the objects do not impel us to acquire them. The impulse of attachment creates incontrovertible urge to obtain them. It does not imply complete, or even partial, renouncement of the perishable objects. They are indispensable to sustain life and livelihood. The perishable objects are not to be blamed. The relevant point is that the attachment to perishable objects, impelled by selfish-will, internalizes (Chapter VI-2) attachment to keep us hanging in an unbalanced inner self—which impairs our welfare. These observations occasion to work on the micro approach to human welfare.

The micro approach to welfare stands on the premise that the use of the impulse of attachment to perishables can improve the welfare of every individual. The stock and flow of perishable objects is not to be disturbed. They contain inputs to sustain production and consumption. The impulse of attachment is nature born, hence out of reach of human manipulation. But work is a double-edged weapon (i) to cleanse the inside world of an individual from the restrictive impact of attachment and (ii) contribute to their welfare in an aggregative sense, through the use of perishable inputs. At the same time, leave (Chapter VII-4) a residue of absolute contentment beyond the reach of the active feeling of happiness gathered by gratification of the senses. We have considered at length how work propelled by the spirit of selfless service (VII-2) and the spirit of sacrificial work (Chapter VII-3) can respectively minimize the internalization of attachment and maximize its externalization. The compelling force of the spirit to benefit others is inestimable. In contrast, the amount of available inputs for production and consumption is estimable. The impact of limited availability of inputs becomes more acute because of an individual's budget constraint. The spirit is an extremely effective device to influence the working of the world inside and outside oneself. The commitment to use the available means by each individual to the betterment of others ensures an ordinal measure of welfare to every individual equal to the sum total of the sacrifices made by others. In comparison to it, the accomplishment of work born of selfish-will contributes a much lower ordinal amount of welfare.

Now we can go in search of the test of welfare contributed by the art (Chapter VII-4) of working. It is asserted that work born of selfish-will gratifies happiness imparted by nature born triad of propensities. The accruing happiness can be ascribed either as contributed by (Verse 18-36-37) the propensity to purity, or by the propensity (Verse 18-38) to passion, or by the propensity (Verse 18-39) to passivity. Let us consider the nature of happiness (Verse 6-21 & 6-22) contributed by the triad of propensities. The happiness of passion depends upon the perishables made available by the order existing outside oneself. An individual actualizes happiness by self-indulgence through the use of five senses. One helplessly accepts utter dependence on the size, composition, and time-shape of availability of perishable goods. The accrued happiness is subject to cycle of contact and separation causing unstable mental states. The happiness of passivity is born of sleep, indolence and neglect. The happiness of passivity makes a direct encroachment on consciousness. The brightness of insight and foresight in intelligence gradually sinks in the fading strength of consciousness. The happiness of purity is born out of delight in intelligence. The delight appears, to disappear, to reappear in intelligence, which is a pseudo-alive entity—that is enlivened by the Self. The happiness of purity although springs from attachment-disembodied thought contents of activity is seldom everlasting and is attainable after a long practice. In any case, the happiness imparted by the triad of propensities are short-lived. It is born of contact with entities partially or totally devoid of consciousness. The double-edged weapon of work not only contributes to welfare in an aggregate sense, but also at the level of individuals. The spirit of sacrificial work (Chapter VII-5) also leaves a remainder of balanced inner self.

The attained balanced inner self is associated with stable contentment or (Verse 2-55) enduring non-appearance of discontent. The cessation of internalization of attachment and maximization of its externalization outside oneself saps the repercussions of desire and work born of selfish-will. It consequently, one experiences that he has (Verse 3-17) no unfinished work to do, no keenness to know and no longing to have something more. It does not mean that the attained welfare puts an end to the urge to action. This is not so. The propensity to passion born urge to action, untainted by selfish-will, tends to arouse public spirit and social conscience. The size and composition of work portfolio (Verse 2-11) is bound to increase and diversify as impelled by attachment-disembodied thought contents of activity. This is for the reason that the urge to work ceases to be guided by desire born of selfish-will, or attachment-embodied thought content of activity. Now it is underlined by, considerateness and generosity incited by the spirit of sacrificial work. This is the acid test of welfare. It is achieved by the thought and action engineered by an individual himself. This is the legacy of perpetually maintained balanced inner self. It yields lasting contentment which belittles (Verse 6-21 & 6-22) all kinds of happiness infused by the triad of propensities. This is because of the innate (Verse 2-40) characteristics of the attained balanced inner self. In the first place, once the eagerness to achieve balanced inner self germinates, it tends to be everlasting. The impatience for something self-existent subsist on its own nature. Secondly, since the aim is to establish intelligence in balanced inner self is devoid of longing for the return from action, its attainment never yields undesirable results. Finally, the attained balanced inner self steeps one into immunity from the ceaseless appearance of agreeable and disagreeable circumstances. Both in life and livelihood. The notable aspect is that is, the stream of active consciousness is stripped of the thought out currents of passion. The stream overflowing with purity pushes intelligence near and nearer to ultimate self-existent entity—the Self. The Self begins to precept the working of the instruments (Verse 6-5) contained in the domain or activity through the intelligence. The working of the domain itself generates enduring contentment, peace and equanimity.

* * *

GLOSSARY

Attachment—The impulse of attachment, born of the propensity to passion, generates likes, agreeability, inclination and usefulness for the objects of attachment. The objects could be thoughts, body, people, work, events, situation, commodities etc. The likes merge into attraction, and attraction into attachment and attachment into psychic fixation.

Aversion—The impulse of aversion is the obverse side of attachment. This is for the reason that taste and distaste, selection and rejection, inclination and disinclination go together.

Action—The human activity is postulated to be evidenced by one's, own thoughts, speech and efforts. Accordingly, we distinguish between the thought and effort contents of activity. The quality of the thought contents is all that matters. The effort content signifies action without thought. The thought content is the determinant of the effort content of activity.

Balanced Inner Self—The term inner self refers to the triad of instruments of activity, namely, the ego, intelligence and the mind. The inner self immune from completion (non-completion) of work, receipt (non-receipt) of returns, joy (sorrow), agreeable (non-agreeable) circumstances defines the balanced inner self. The concept is indicative of poise or complete psychic equilibrium. It is postulated that the acquired balance matures into natural balanced inner self. The complete sameness between the inner self and the Self denotes the natural balanced state of the inner self.

Constrained-concern—The concern with respect to one's body, the Self, entities contained inside and outside the body—people, their activities and produce of their activities define the orbit of and individual's concern. The concerns precepted by attachment and egoism degenerate into 'constrained—concern'.

The concerns delivered from the bind of attachment and egoism are 'unconstrained-concern'.

Constrained activity—the constrained and unconstrained concerns respectively conclude in constrained—activity and unconstrained activity.

Domain of Activity—The human existence consists of his body and soul (or the Self). The body is called the domain of activity endowed by nature. And the Self supposed to be a fraction of the Supreme—Self is the animator of the domain. The domain contains a variety of instruments of activity. All human activities are accomplished by and in nature. The Self is postulated to be beyond nature and the creations of nature.

Ego—is born of the union of the body and the Self. As such one portion of ego is endowed with and the other portion is devoid of consciousness. The former ego refers to the self—sense of being-ness. It is natural ego. The other portion of ego is acquired one. The acquired ego embodies the attributes of entities other than the Self. Accordingly, ego can accommodate either attachment—embodied or attachment-disembodied impulses, which give rise to non-neutral or neutral tendencies in the domain of activity.

Human capital—The existence of human being comprises his body and the soul (the self). The Self is supposed to be a fraction of the Supreme-Self. It infuses life energy, knowledge, happiness, insight, and foresight as inputs to animate the domain of activity. The inputs supplied by the Self define the notion or 'primary human capital'. The instruments contained in the body (domain of activity) are endowed by nature. The inputs supplied by nature define the 'secondary human capital'.

Individual—For analytical purpose the notion of a micro unit signifies an individual as a unit.

I-ness—The living soul knows the body, the senses, mind and intelligence as his own. This is mere an assumption. This is for the reason that the living soul and all other entities belong to completely different genus. Yet the living soul on occasion identifies 'I' as the body. This is I-ness. And at other time the living soul treats the body as mine. This is the notion of mine-ness.

Instrument of activity—The instruments contained in the body are (i) organs of action, (ii) organs of perception called the senses (iii) and the mind, intelligence and ego. The action organs and the senses are called external instruments of activity. And the remaining three entities are labeled as the internal instruments of activity (or the inner self). The internal instruments precept the working of the external instruments of activity.

The input & Output-mix—The instruments contained in the body function as a machine—action without thought. The instruments are unmindful of the inputs received from the Self, ego and the triad of propensities. The instruments are also unmindful of the produced output-mix. The thought contents of activity constitute the ingredients of the input and output-mix.

Knowledge—Refers to the comprehension the discerns the difference between self-existent (non-existent), perishable (non-perishable), domain of activity (its animator). The domain is beset with flaws and imperfections. It is also subject to ceaseless change. But the Self is beyond change. The Self is the knower and animator of the domain. The ignorance about the difference between the Self and other entities is non-knowledge.

Thus the thoughts contents of activity which decrease the self-senses of bodily consciousness and increase insight, foresight and rational thinking are defined as knowledge. The thoughts like anger, arrogance, excessive pride of one's individuality etc, which enhance the self-sense and irrationality are non-knowledge.

Micro order—The notion conceptualizes the beingness of an individual. The body and soul (the Self) constituting the order belong to different genus—one is endowed by nature and the other is supposed to be a fraction of the Supreme-Self. The interaction between the selected variables (the Self (S), Ego (E), Instruments of activity (I) and triad of propensities (P), give and insight into the working of the micro order.

Neutral & Non-neutral thought contents of activity—The attachment—embodied ego causes the instruments contained in the domain to produce thought contents of activity tainted by the impulses of attachment and aversion. These thought contents back fire into the domain to upset the spontaneous functioning of the micro order. These thought contents are in essence non-neutral. In contrast, the attachment-disembodied ego diffuses tendencies to restore the natural functioning of the micro order by generating neutral thought contents of activity.

Non-involvement—The concept requires one to imbibe a tangential attitude to work before, during and after the completion of work. This is necessary to wipe out the incidence of subjective constraints caused by attachment to the various aspects of work, particularly attachment to the return from work.

Propensities—The triad of propensities is nature born. The propensities are those of passion, passivity and purity. The thought currents of passion activate desire born of selfish-will and urge to activity. The thought currents of passivity deactivate action but not the desires born of selfish-will. The thought currents of purity enlighten the sequence of activity before, during and after the completion of work.

While the thought currents of passion and passivity intensify the impulse of attachment and impair wisdom, the thought of purity deliver one from attachment and brighten wisdom in intelligence.

Propensity-mix—The decision of and individual motivated by selfish-will incites the propensity to passion or passivity to assume a lead, hence enforce a retreat of the thought currents of purity. The propensity-mix driven by unselfish motive fosters the thought currents of purity equal to or more than in strength as compared to the thought currents of passion, hence causing a retreat of the thought currents of passivity.

Soul (or the Self)—The principle of life, feeling, thought and action in man, regarded as distinct entity separate from the body, and commonly held to be separable in existence from the body. It is also called an alive-entity.

Self-existent—Existing by its own nature or essence—independent of any cause. The Self is the only self-existent entity. The entities other than the Self are non-existent in nature. They are devoid of consciousness and subject to ceaseless change and destruction.

Subjective constraints—The attachment-embodied (or non-neutral) thought contents of activity crystallize into subjective constraints. In essence the cause and consequence of constraints both are subjective. The binding power of attachment creates subjective constraints in multiple directions with varying degree of its restrictive impact.

*   *   *